Henry Van Dyke

Responsive Readings

Selected from the Bible and arranged under subjects for common worship

Henry Van Dyke

Responsive Readings
Selected from the Bible and arranged under subjects for common worship

ISBN/EAN: 9783337170233

Printed in Europe, USA, Canada, Australia, Japan

Cover: Foto ©Lupo / pixelio.de

More available books at **www.hansebooks.com**

RESPONSIVE READINGS

SELECTED FROM THE BIBLE AND
ARRANGED UNDER SUBJECTS
FOR COMMON WORSHIP

BY

HENRY VAN DYKE

BOSTON, U.S.A., AND LONDON
GINN & COMPANY, PUBLISHERS
1895

COPYRIGHT, 1895,
BY HENRY VAN DYKE.

ALL RIGHTS RESERVED.

TYPOGRAPHY BY J. S. CUSHING & CO., NORWOOD, MASS., U.S.A.
PRESSWORK BY GINN & CO., BOSTON, MASS., U.S.A.

PREFACE.

THIS book was originally prepared, by request, for the Chapel of Harvard University, where it is now in use. It has been revised and enlarged, in the hope that it may supply a real need in the religious services of other colleges and schools, and of churches which desire to make the responsive reading of Scripture a brief, simple, and profitable part of Common Worship.

The selections have been made and arranged with the following objects in view: To give a wider range to the service by including appropriate passages for antiphonal reading from all parts of the Bible; to omit the imprecatory Psalms; to make each selection complete in itself, with a central thought, and not to attempt a mosaic of disconnected passages; to divide the verses only when it helps to make the meaning clear and to keep the portion read by the people from being too long; to vary the length of the selections so that it may be easy to find one to fit a short service when necessary; and to arrange the readings in relation to the great truths of religion, so that they may be instructive and helpful to faith and life.

The Lord's Prayer, The Apostles' Creed, and the Ten Commandments have been included in the book; a response to be sung after the Commandments, and a doxology for use at the close of the Responsive Readings, have been added for those who may wish to have these forms of worship in a single volume. It is sent forth with the sincere petition that the Holy Spirit of liberty and order may make it of service

AD MAJOREM GLORIAM DEI.

LIST OF SUBJECTS.

———•◦•———

                                                                      PAGE

I. UNIVERSAL PRAISE. (Selections 1–5.)
    1. Praise in Heaven and Earth......... 1
    2. A New Song...................... 2
    3. The Gladness of Worship........... 4
    4. Sing unto the Lord, All the Earth.... 4
    5. Let all the People Praise Thee....... 6

II. THE TRUE GOD. (Selections 6–10.)
    6. The Lord Reigneth................ 7
    7. The Vanity of Idols............... 8
    8. The Creator of the Ends of the Earth 10
    9. In God We Live................... 12
    10. Our Lord is above all Gods......... 14

III. OF GOD'S GLORY. (Selections 11–16.)
    11. How Manifold are Thy Works....... 16
    12. How Excellent is Thy Name 18
    13. The Earth is the Lord's............ 20
    14. Worship the Lord in the Beauty of
         Holiness 21
    15. Sing unto God, ye Kingdoms........ 22
    16. The King of all the Earth.......... 24

IV. OF GOD'S RIGHTEOUSNESS. (Selections 17–20.)
    17. The Law of the Lord is Perfect..... 26
    18. Verity and Judgment are His Works.. 28

List of Subjects.

		PAGE
19.	His Name is Holy.......	29
20.	Thy Judgments are Good.	30

V. OF GOD'S GOODNESS. (Selections 21–28.)

21.	For He is Good...................	32
22.	The Loving-kindness of the Lord....	34
23.	Every Day Will I Bless Thee........	35
24.	Chastisement and Deliverance.......	37
25.	God's Wonders in the Deep........	39
26.	Thou Visitest the Earth...........	40
27.	National Blessings.................	42
28.	O Give Thanks....................	43

VI. OF GOD'S MERCY. (Selections 29–39.)

29.	His Mercy Endureth Forever........	46
30.	Forget Not All His Benefits	47
31.	How Excellent is Thy Loving-kindness	50
32.	The Giver of the Heart's Desire.....	51
33.	The Lord hath Respect unto the Lowly	52
34.	Thou Tellest My Wanderings........	53
35.	Verily God hath Heard Me..........	54
36.	I Love the Lord...................	56
37.	In the Shadow of Thy Wings.......	58
38.	The Great Helper.................	59
39.	This Poor Man Cried..............	60

VII. OF GOD'S FAITHFULNESS. (Selections 40–49.)

40.	The Covenant.....................	63
41.	Remember the Days of Old.........	64
42.	The Lord is Our Defence...........	66
43.	The People of His Pasture..........	67
44.	I will Declare Thy Name...........	68
45.	Blessed is the Nation..............	70

List of Subjects.

	PAGE
46. We have Waited for Him...............	71
47. He hath not Dealt so with Any Nation	73
48. A Morning Prayer...................	75
49. Serve the Lord with Gladness........	76

VIII. OF GOD'S WISDOM. (Selections 50–57.)

50. The Unsearchable God..............	78
51. The Searcher of Hearts	79
52. Where shall Wisdom be Found?....	81
53. Search for Her as for Hid Treasure ..	82
54. She is More Precious than Rubies....	83
55. Doth not Wisdom Cry?............	85
56. Good Doctrine.....................	87
57. So Teach Us to Number Our Days...	88

IX. CHRIST AND HIS KINGDOM. (Selections 58–81.)

58. Thou art My Son	91
59. The Heir of All Things............	92
60. Fairer than the Children of Men.....	94
61. Men Shall be Blessed in Him.......	96
62. The Magnificat.....................	99
63. The Benedictus.....................	100
64. The True Oblations.................	101
65. The Promised Light	102
66. Behold My Servant.................	104
67. The First-born of All Creation.......	106
68. Surely He Hath Borne Our Griefs....	108
69. Perfect through Sufferings...........	110
70. Prepare Ye the Way of the Lord.....	112
71. The Messenger of Good Tidings.....	114
72. The Spirit of the Lord shall Rest upon Him......................	115
73. The Lord hath Anointed Me........	117

List of Subjects.

		PAGE
74.	The Covenant of Peace	119
75.	Our Peace	121
76.	The Joy of the Whole Earth	123
77.	Great Shall be the Peace of Thy Children	124
78.	They Shall Obtain Joy and Gladness	125
79.	Arise, Shine, for Thy Light is Come	127
80.	The Gospel of Peace	129
81.	The Invitation	131

X. THE SPIRIT OF LIFE. (Selections 82–86.)

82.	The Spirit Beareth Witness	134
83.	The Law of the Spirit	136
84.	The Ministration of the Spirit	137
85.	The Fruits of the Spirit	139
86.	The Unity of the Spirit	141

XI. TRUE RELIGION. (Selections 87–90.)

87.	The Fast that God hath Chosen	143
88.	God shall Judge His People	145
89.	Pure Religion and Undefiled	146
90.	Add to Your Faith Virtue	148

XII. THE LAW OF GOD. (Selections 91–103.)

91.	Blessed are the Undefiled	150
92.	Thy Testimonies are My Delight	151
93.	The Way of Truth	152
94.	This is My Comfort	153
95.	Teach me Good Judgment	155
96.	Thy Word is Settled in Heaven	156
97.	A Light unto My Path	157
98.	Order my Steps in Thy Word	158
99.	Thy Word is Very Pure	159
100.	Consider how I Love Thy Precepts	160
101.	My Heart Standeth in Awe	162

		PAGE
102.	Let Thine Hand Help Me	163
103.	Return unto the Lord	164

XIII. PENITENCE AND PARDON. (Selections 104–114.)

104.	Cleanse Me from My Sin	166
105.	There is Forgiveness with Thee	167
106.	A Prayer for the Penitent	168
107.	If We Confess our Sins	170
108.	Pardon mine Iniquity, for it is Great	171
109.	Deliver me from my Transgressions	173
110.	Enter not into Judgment	174
111.	I hope in Thy Word	176
112.	Thou hast Covered all their Sin	177
113.	The Blessedness of Pardon	178
114.	The Righteousness of God which is by Faith	180

XIV. THE JOY OF RELIGION. (Selections 115–126.)

115.	The Lord is my Shepherd	182
116.	Strong Son of God, Immortal Love	183
117.	Trials and Consolations	184
118.	Be Mindful of His Covenant	186
119.	Fear not, O Land	187
120.	Therefore My Heart is Glad	188
121.	A New Name	190
122.	Rejoice in the Lord	191
123.	The Righteous shall Flourish	192
124.	We Believe and therefore Speak	193
125.	Peace with God	195
126.	Blessed are They that Dwell in Thy House	196

List of Subjects.

	PAGE
XV. TRUST AND CONFIDENCE. (Selections 127-146.)	
127. God Our Refuge	198
128. As the Mountains are round about Jerusalem	199
129. Be Thou My Strong Rock	201
130. A Shield to all that Trust Thee	203
131. Preserve My Soul	204
132. The Lord is on Our Side	206
133. I Waited Patiently for the Lord	207
134. I have Trusted in Thy Mercy	209
135. Thou Knewest My Path	210
136. In His Favour is Life	211
137. Thou Makest Me Dwell in Safety	213
138. Under the Shadow of the Almighty	214
139. The Rock that is Higher than I	216
140. I shall not be Moved	217
141. The Lord is Thy Keeper	218
142. Is not God in the Height of Heaven?	219
143. He Beholdeth all the Sons of Men	221
144. A Prayer in Trouble	222
145. My Fortress and My Deliverer	224
146. Happy is that People Whose God is the Lord	226
XVI. COURAGE AND HOPE. (Selections 147-160.)	
147. The Armour of God	228
148. Be of Good Courage	229
149. Hope in God	231
150. Watch and Be Sober	233
151. Always Confident	234
152. Let us Run with Patience	236
153. Grace to Help in Time of Need	238
154. The New Covenant	239

		PAGE
155.	I shall yet Praise Him	240
156.	Forget not the Lord	242
157.	Keep His Commandments	244
158.	The Blessings of Obedience	246
159.	A Vow of Service	248
160.	A Vow Performed and Rewarded	249

XVII. SERVICE AND REWARD. (Selections 161–174.)

161.	Good Resolutions	251
162.	An Upright Character	252
163.	Praise of a Good Life	253
164.	The Reward of Righteousness	254
165.	The Two Paths	256
166.	Trust in the Lord and Do Good	257
167.	The Happy Man	258
168.	The Steps of a Good Man	259
169.	The Righteous shall Endure	260
170.	Judgment according to Truth	262
171.	The Vanity of Riches	263
172.	The Fulfilling of the Law	265
173.	Acceptable Sacrifice	266
174.	The Proof of Our Ministry	268

XVIII. LOVE AND BROTHERHOOD. (Selections 175–180.)

175.	The Peace of Jerusalem	270
176.	Unity in Christ	271
177.	The Greatest of These is Charity	273
178.	Love is of God	275
179.	The Sons of God	277
180.	Members One of Another	279

		PAGE

XIX. COUNSELS OF PERFECTION. (Selections 181–191.)

- 181. The Blessings of Jesus............. 281
- 182. The Life of Jesus in Us............ 282
- 183. The Mind of Christ................ 283
- 184. Follow That Which is Good......... 285
- 185. Be Not Weary in Well Doing....... 286
- 186. Truth, Peace, Purity, Forgiveness.... 287
- 187. The Children of Light.............. 288
- 188. Let Us Glory in the Lord 289
- 189. According to Jesus Christ 291
- 190. Love and Light.................... 292
- 191. Consider Christ................... 293

XX. THE RISEN LIFE. (Selections 192–200.)

- 192. Now is Christ Risen from the Dead.. 296
- 193. Risen with Christ 297
- 194. In Newness of Life 300
- 195. A Lively Hope.................... 301
- 196. The Victory over Death........... 302
- 197. Our House which is from Heaven... 304
- 198. The Blessedness of the Redeemed... 305
- 199. The Holy City.................... 307
- 200. The River of Water of Life........ 308

THE LORD'S PRAYER.

OUR FATHER, WHICH ART IN HEAVEN,
    HALLOWED BE THY NAME,
    THY KINGDOM COME,
THY WILL BE DONE, IN EARTH, AS IT IS IN HEAVEN.

GIVE US THIS DAY OUR DAILY BREAD,
    AND FORGIVE US OUR DEBTS,
    AS WE FORGIVE OUR DEBTORS,
    AND LEAD US NOT INTO TEMPTATION,
    BUT DELIVER US FROM EVIL;
FOR THINE IS THE KINGDOM,
AND THE POWER, AND THE GLORY, FOR EVER.
                                  AMEN.

THE APOSTLES' CREED.

I BELIEVE in God the Father Almighty, Maker of Heaven and earth:

And in Jesus Christ His only Son our Lord; who was conceived by the Holy Ghost; born of the Virgin Mary; suffered under Pontius Pilate; was crucified, dead, and buried; He descended into Hell; the third day He rose again from the dead; He ascended into Heaven; and sitteth on the right hand of God the Father Almighty; from thence He shall come to judge the quick and the dead.

I believe in the Holy Ghost; the holy Catholic Church; the Communion of Saints; the Forgiveness of sins; the Resurrection of the body; and the Life everlasting. Amen.

THE TEN COMMANDMENTS.

I AM the Lord thy God, which have brought thee out of the land of Egypt, out of the house of bondage.

I. Thou shalt have no other gods before me.

II. Thou shalt not make unto thee any graven image, or any likeness of anything that is in heaven above, or that is in the earth beneath, or that is in the water under the earth: thou shalt not bow down thyself to them, nor serve them: for I the Lord thy God am a jealous God, visiting the iniquity of the fathers upon the children unto the third and fourth generation of them that hate me; and shewing mercy unto thousands of them that love me and keep my commandments.

III. Thou shalt not take the name of the Lord thy God in vain, for the Lord will not hold him guiltless that taketh his name in vain.

IV. Remember the Sabbath day to keep it holy; six days shalt thou labour, and do all thy work; but the seventh day is the Sabbath of the Lord thy God; in it thou shalt not do any work, thou, nor thy son, nor thy daughter, thy man-servant, nor thy maid-servant, nor thy cattle, nor thy stranger that is within thy gates: for in six days the Lord made heaven and earth, the sea, and all that in them is, and rested the seventh day; Wherefore the Lord blessed the Sabbath day, and hallowed it.

V. Honour thy father and thy mother, that thy days may be long upon the land which the Lord thy God giveth thee.

VI. Thou shalt not kill.

VII. Thou shalt not commit adultery.

VIII. Thou shalt not steal.

IX. Thou shalt not bear false witness against thy neighbour.

X. Thou shalt not covet thy neighbour's house, thou shalt not covet thy neighbour's wife, nor his man-servant, nor his maid-servant, nor his ox, nor his ass, nor anything that is thy neighbour's.

Response.

Gloria Patri.

GLORY be to the Father, and | to the | Son, |
　　And | to the | Holy | Ghost ;
As it was in the beginning, is now, and | ever | shall be, |
　　World | without | end. A- | men.

RESPONSIVE READINGS.

I.

UNIVERSAL PRAISE.

First Selection.

Praise in Heaven and Earth.

PRAISE ye the Lord.
✠ Praise ye the Lord from the heavens : praise him in the heights.

Praise ye him, all his angels : praise ye him, all his hosts.

✠ Praise ye him, sun and moon : praise him, all ye stars of light.

Praise him, ye heavens of heavens, and ye waters that *be* above the heavens.

✠ Let them praise the name of the Lord : for he commanded, and they were created.

He hath also established them for ever and ever : he hath made a decree which shall not pass.

✠ Praise the Lord from the earth, ye dragons and all deeps :

Fire, and hail; snow, and vapours; stormy wind fulfilling his word:

✠ Mountains, and all hills; fruitful trees, and all cedars:

Beasts, and all cattle; creeping things, and flying fowl:

✠ Kings of the earth, and all people; princes, and all judges of the earth:

Both young men, and maidens; old men, and children:

✠ Let them praise the name of the LORD: for his name alone is excellent; his glory *is* above the earth and heaven.

He also exalteth the horn of his people, the praise of all his saints; *even* of the children of Israel, a people near unto him.

✠ Praise ye the LORD.

Psalm cxlviii. 1–14.

Second Selection.

A New Song.

O SING unto the LORD a new song: for he hath done marvellous things: his right hand, and his holy arm, hath gotten him the victory.

✠ The LORD hath made known his salvation: his righteousness hath he openly shewed in the sight of the heathen.

He hath remembered his mercy and his truth toward the house of Israel: all the ends of the earth have seen the salvation of our God.

✣ Make a joyful noise unto the Lord, all the earth: make a loud noise, and rejoice, and sing praise.

Sing unto the Lord with the harp; with the harp, and the voice of a psalm.

✣ With trumpets and sound of cornet make a joyful noise before the Lord, the King.

Let the sea roar, and the fulness thereof; the world, and they that dwell therein.

✣ Let the floods clap *their* hands: let the hills be joyful together

Before the Lord; for he cometh to judge the earth: with righteousness shall he judge the world, and the people with equity.

Psalm xcviii. 1–9.

Third Selection.

The Gladness of Worship.

PRAISE ye the Lord.
✠ Praise God in his sanctuary: praise him in the firmament of his power.

Praise him for his mighty acts: praise him according to his excellent greatness.

✠ Praise him with the sound of the trumpet: praise him with the psaltery and harp.

Praise him with the timbrel and dance: praise him with stringed instruments and organs.

✠ Praise him upon the loud cymbals: praise him upon the high-sounding cymbals.

Let every thing that hath breath praise the Lord.

✠ Praise ye the Lord.   *Psalm cl. 1-6.*

Fourth Selection.

Sing unto the Lord, All the Earth.

SING unto the Lord, all the earth; shew forth from day to day his salvation.

✠ Declare his glory among the heathen; his marvellous works among all nations.

For great *is* the Lord, and greatly to be praised : he also *is* to be feared above all gods.

✠ For all the gods of the people *are* idols : but the Lord made the heavens.

Glory and honour *are* in his presence ; strength and gladness *are* in his place.

✠ Give unto the Lord, ye kindreds of the people, give unto the Lord glory and strength.

Give unto the Lord the glory *due* unto his name : bring an offering, and come before him : worship the Lord in the beauty of holiness.

✠ Fear before him, all the earth : the world also shall be stable, that it be not moved.

Let the heavens be glad, and let the earth rejoice : and let *men* say among the nations, The Lord reigneth.

✠ Let the sea roar, and the fulness thereof : let the fields rejoice, and all that *is* therein.

Then shall the trees of the wood sing out at the presence of the Lord, because he cometh to judge the earth.

✠ O give thanks unto the Lord ; for *he is* good ; for his mercy *endureth* for ever.

And say ye, Save us, O God of our salvation, and gather us together, and deliver us from the heathen, that we may give thanks to thy holy name, *and* glory in thy praise.

✠ Blessed *be* the LORD God of Israel for ever and ever. And all the people said, Amen, and praised the LORD.

1 *Chronicles* xvi. 23-36.

Fifth Selection.

Let all the People Praise Thee.

GOD be merciful unto us, and bless us; *and* cause his face to shine upon us.

✠ That thy way may be known upon earth, thy saving health among all nations.

Let the people praise thee, O God; let all the people praise thee.

✠ O let the nations be glad and sing for joy: for thou shalt judge the people righteously, and govern the nations upon earth.

Let the people praise thee, O God; let all the people praise thee.

✠ *Then* shall the earth yield her increase; *and* God, *even* our own God, shall bless us.

God shall bless us, and all the ends of the earth shall fear him. *Psalm* lxvii. 1-7.

II.

THE TRUE GOD.

Sixth Selection.

The Lord Reigneth.

THE LORD reigneth; let the earth rejoice; let the multitude of isles be glad *thereof.*

✠ Clouds and darkness *are* round about him: righteousness and judgment *are* the habitation of his throne.

A fire goeth before him, and burneth up his enemies round about.

✠ His lightnings enlightened the world: the earth saw, and trembled.

The hills melted like wax at the presence of the LORD, at the presence of the LORD of the whole earth.

✠ The heavens declare his righteousness, and all the people see his glory.

Confounded be all they that serve graven images, that boast themselves of idols: worship him, all *ye* gods.

✠ Zion heard, and was glad; and the daughters of Judah rejoiced because of thy judgments, O Lord.

For thou, Lord, *art* high above all the earth: thou art exalted far above all gods.

✠ Ye that love the Lord, hate evil.

He preserveth the souls of his saints; he delivereth them out of the hand of the wicked.

✠ Light is sown for the righteous, and gladness for the upright in heart.

Rejoice in the Lord, ye righteous; and give thanks at the remembrance of his holiness.

Psalm xcvii. 1–12.

Seventh Selection.

The Vanity of Idols.

NOT unto us, O Lord, not unto us, but unto thy name give glory, for thy mercy, *and* for thy truth's sake.

✠ Wherefore should the heathen say, Where *is* now their God?

But our God *is* in the heavens: he hath done whatsoever he pleased.

✠ Their idols *are* silver and gold, the work of men's hands.

They have mouths, but they speak not: eyes have they, but they see not:

✠ They have ears, but they hear not: noses have they, but they smell not:

They have hands, but they handle not: feet have they, but they walk not: neither speak they through their throat.

✠ They that make them are like unto them; *so is* every one that trusteth in them.

O Israel, trust thou in the Lord: he *is* their help and their shield.

✠ O house of Aaron, trust in the Lord: he *is* their help and their shield.

Ye that fear the Lord, trust in the Lord: he *is* their help and their shield.

✠ The Lord hath been mindful of us: he will bless *us;*

He will bless the house of Israel; he will bless the house of Aaron.

✠ He will bless them that fear the Lord, *both* small and great.

The Lord shall increase you more and more, you and your children.

✠ Ye *are* blessed of the Lord which made heaven and earth.

The heaven, *even* the heavens, *are* the Lord's: but the earth hath he given to the children of men.

✠ The dead praise not the Lord, neither any that go down into silence.

But we will bless the Lord from this time forth and for evermore. Praise the Lord.

Psalm cxv. 1-18.

Eighth Selection.

The Creator of the Ends of the Earth.

To whom then will ye liken God? or what likeness will ye compare unto him?

✠ The workman melteth a graven image, and the goldsmith spreadeth it over with gold, and casteth silver chains.

He that *is* so impoverished that he hath no oblation chooseth a tree *that* will not rot; he seeketh unto him a cunning workman to prepare a graven image, *that* shall not be moved.

✠ Have ye not known? have ye not heard? hath it not been told you from the beginning? have ye not understood from the foundations of the earth?

It is he that sitteth upon the circle of the earth, and the inhabitants thereof *are* as grasshoppers; that stretcheth out the heavens as a curtain, and spreadeth them out as a tent to dwell in:

✢ That bringeth the princes to nothing; he maketh the judges of the earth as vanity.

Yea, they shall not be planted; yea, they shall not be sown: yea, their stock shall not take root in the earth: and he shall also blow upon them, and they shall wither, and the whirlwind shall take them away as stubble.

✢ To whom then will ye liken me, or shall I be equal? saith the Holy One.

Lift up your eyes on high, and behold who hath created these *things*, that bringeth out their host by number: he calleth them all by names by the greatness of his might, for that *he is* strong in power; not one faileth.

✢ Why sayest thou, O Jacob, and speakest, O Israel, My way is hid from the LORD, and my judgment is passed over from my God?

Hast thou not known? hast thou not heard, *that* the everlasting God, the Lord, the Creator of the ends of the earth, fainteth not, neither is weary? *there is* no searching of his understanding.

✠ He giveth power to the faint; and to *them that have* no might he increaseth strength.

Even the youths shall faint and be weary, and the young men shall utterly fall:

✠ But they that wait upon the Lord shall renew *their* strength; they shall mount up with wings as eagles;

They shall run, and not be weary; *and* they shall walk, and not faint.

Isaiah xl. 18-31.

Ninth Selection.

In God We Live.

GOD that made the world and all things therein, seeing that he is Lord of heaven and earth, dwelleth not in temples made with hands;

✠ Neither is worshipped with men's hands, as though he needed any thing, seeing he giveth to all life, and breath, and all things;

And hath made of one blood all nations of men for to dwell on all the face of the earth, and hath determined the times before appointed, and the bounds of their habitation;

✣ That they should seek the Lord, if haply they might feel after him, and find him, though he be not far from every one of us:

For in him we live, and move, and have our being; as certain also of your own poets have said, For we are also his offspring.

✣ Forasmuch then as we are the offspring of God, we ought not to think that the Godhead is like unto gold, or silver, or stone, graven by art and man's device.

And the times of this ignorance God winked at; but now commandeth all men everywhere to repent:

✣ Because he hath appointed a day, in the which he will judge the world in righteousness by *that* man whom he hath ordained;

Whereof he hath given assurance unto all *men*, in that he hath raised him from the dead.

Acts xvii. 24–31.

Tenth Selection.

Our Lord is above all Gods.

PRAISE ye the Lord. Praise ye the name of the Lord; praise *him*, O ye servants of the Lord.

✠ Ye that stand in the house of the Lord, in the courts of the house of our God,

Praise the Lord; for the Lord *is* good; sing praises unto his name; for *it is* pleasant.

✠ For the Lord hath chosen Jacob unto himself, *and* Israel for his peculiar treasure.

For I know that the Lord *is* great, and *that* our Lord *is* above all gods.

✠ The idols of the heathen *are* silver and gold, the work of men's hands.

They have mouths, but they speak not; eyes have they, but they see not;

✠ They have ears, but they hear not; neither is there *any* breath in their mouths.

They that make them are like unto them; *so is* every one that trusteth in them.

✠ Bless the Lord, O house of Israel: bless the Lord, O house of Aaron:

Bless the Lord, O house of Levi: ye that fear the Lord, bless the Lord.

✠ Blessed be the Lord out of Zion, which dwelleth at Jerusalem. Praise ye the Lord.

Psalm cxxxv. 1–5, 15–21.

III.

OF GOD'S GLORY.

―•◦•―

Eleventh Selection.

How Manifold are Thy Works.

BLESS the Lord, O my soul. O Lord my God, thou art very great; thou art clothed with honour and majesty.

✠ Who coverest *thyself* with light as *with* a garment: who stretchest out the heavens like a curtain:

Who layeth the beams of his chambers in the waters: who maketh the clouds his chariot: who walketh upon the wings of the wind:

✠ Who maketh his angels spirits; his ministers a flaming fire:

Who laid the foundations of the earth, *that* it should not be removed for ever.

✠ Thou coveredst it with the deep as *with* a garment: the waters stood above the mountains.

At thy rebuke they fled; at the voice of thy thunder they hasted away.

✠ They go up by the mountain; they go down by the valleys unto the place which thou hast founded for them.

Thou hast set a bound that they may not pass over; that they turn not again to cover the earth.

✠ He sendeth the springs into the valleys, *which* run among the hills.

They give drink to every beast of the field: the wild asses quench their thirst.

✠ By them shall the fowls of the heaven have their habitation, *which* sing among the branches.

He watereth the hills from his chambers: the earth is satisfied with the fruit of thy works.

✠ He causeth the grass to grow for the cattle, and herb for the service of man:

That he may bring forth food out of the earth; and wine *that* maketh glad the heart of man, *and* oil to make *his* face to shine, and bread *which* strengtheneth man's heart.

✠ The trees of the Lord are full *of sap:* the cedars of Lebanon, which he hath planted;

Where the birds make their nests: *as for* the stork, the fir-trees *are* her house.

✢ The high hills *are* a refuge for the wild goats; *and* the rocks for the conies.

He appointeth the moon for seasons: the sun knoweth his going down.

✢ Thou makest darkness, and it is night: wherein all the beasts of the forest do creep *forth*.

The young lions roar after their prey, and seek their meat from God.

✢ The sun ariseth, they gather themselves together, and lay them down in their dens.

Man goeth forth to his work and to his labour until the evening.

✢ O LORD, how manifold are thy works! in wisdom hast thou made them all: the earth is full of thy riches.

Psalm civ. 1–24.

Twelfth Selection.

How Excellent is Thy Name.

O LORD our Lord, how excellent *is* thy name in all the earth!

✠ Who hast set thy glory above the heavens.

Out of the mouth of babes and sucklings hast thou ordained strength because of thine enemies,

✠ That thou mightest still the enemy and the avenger.

When I consider thy heavens, the work of thy fingers, the moon and the stars, which thou hast ordained;

✠ What is man, that thou art mindful of him? and the son of man, that thou visitest him?

For thou hast made him a little lower than the angels, and hast crowned him with glory and honour.

✠ Thou madest him to have dominion over the works of thy hands;

Thou hast put all *things* under his feet:

✠ All sheep and oxen, yea, and the beasts of the field;

The fowl of the air, and the fish of the sea, *and whatsoever* passeth through the paths of the seas.

✠ O Lord our Lord, how excellent *is* thy name in all the earth!

Psalm viii. 1–9.

Thirteenth Selection.

The Earth is the Lord's.

THE earth *is* the Lord's, and the fulness thereof; the world, and they that dwell therein.

✢ For he hath founded it upon the seas, and established it upon the floods.

Who shall ascend into the hill of the Lord? and who shall stand in his holy place?

✢ He that hath clean hands, and a pure heart; who hath not lifted up his soul unto vanity, nor sworn deceitfully.

He shall receive the blessing from the Lord, and righteousness from the God of his salvation.

✢ This *is* the generation of them that seek him, that seek thy face, O Jacob.

Lift up your heads, O ye gates; and be ye lift up, ye everlasting doors; and the King of glory shall come in.

✢ Who *is* this King of glory?

The Lord strong and mighty, the Lord mighty in battle.

✢ Lift up your heads, O ye gates; even

lift *them* up, ye everlasting doors; and the King of glory shall come in.

Who is this King of glory?

✠ The Lord of hosts, he *is* the King of glory.

Psalm xxiv. 1-10.

Fourteenth Selection.

Worship the Lord in the Beauty of Holiness.

O SING unto the Lord a new song: sing unto the Lord, all the earth.

✠ Sing unto the Lord, bless his name; shew forth his salvation from day to day.

Declare his glory among the heathen, his wonders among all people.

✠ For the Lord *is* great, and greatly to be praised: he *is* to be feared above all gods.

For all the gods of the nations *are* idols: but the Lord made the heavens.

✠ Honour and majesty *are* before him: strength and beauty *are* in his sanctuary.

Give unto the Lord, O ye kindreds of the people, give unto the Lord glory and strength.

✠ Give unto the Lord the glory *due unto*

his name: bring an offering, and come into his courts.

O worship the LORD in the beauty of holiness: fear before him, all the earth.

✠ Say among the heathen *that* the LORD reigneth:

The world also shall be established that it shall not be moved: he shall judge the people righteously.

✠ Let the heavens rejoice, and let the earth be glad; let the sea roar, and the fulness thereof.

Let the field be joyful, and all that *is* therein: then shall all the trees of the wood rejoice before the LORD: for he cometh, for he cometh to judge the earth:

✠ He shall judge the world with righteousness, and the people with his truth.

Psalm xcvi. 1-13.

Fifteenth Selection.

Sing unto God ye Kingdoms.

LET God arise, let his enemies be scattered: let them also that hate him flee before him.

✠ As smoke is driven away, *so* drive

them away: as wax melteth before the fire, *so* let the wicked perish at the presence of God.

But let the righteous be glad; let them rejoice before God: yea, let them exceedingly rejoice.

✠ Sing unto God, sing praises to his name:

Extol him that rideth upon the heavens by his name JAH, and rejoice before him.

✠ A father of the fatherless, and a judge of the widows, *is* God in his holy habitation.

God setteth the solitary in families: he bringeth out those which are bound with chains: but the rebellious dwell in a dry *land*.

✠ O God, when thou wentest forth before thy people, when thou didst march through the wilderness;

The earth shook, the heavens also dropped at the presence of God: *even* Sinai itself *was moved* at the presence of God, the God of Israel.

✠ Sing unto God, ye kingdoms of the earth; O sing praises unto the Lord;

To him that rideth upon the heavens of

heavens, *which were* of old; lo, he doth send out his voice, *and that* a mighty voice.

✠ Ascribe ye strength unto God: his excellency *is* over Israel, and his strength *is* in the clouds.

O God, *thou art* terrible out of thy holy places: the God of Israel *is* he that giveth strength and power unto *his* people. Blessed *be* God.

Psalm lxviii. 1-8, 32-35.

Sixteenth Selection.

The King of all the Earth.

O CLAP your hands, all ye people, shout unto God with the voice of triumph.

✠ For the LORD Most High *is* terrible; *he is* a great King over all the earth.

He shall subdue the people under us, and the nations under our feet.

✠ He shall choose our inheritance for us, the excellency of Jacob whom he loved.

God is gone up with a shout, the LORD with the sound of a trumpet.

✠ Sing praises to God, sing praises: sing praises unto our King, sing praises.

For God *is* the King of all the earth: sing ye praises with understanding.

✠ God reigneth over the heathen: God sitteth upon the throne of his holiness.

The princes of the people are gathered together, *even* the people of the God of Abraham: for the shields of the earth *belong* unto God: he is greatly exalted.

Psalm xlvii. 1–9.

IV.

OF GOD'S RIGHTEOUSNESS.

Seventeenth Selection.

The Law of the Lord is Perfect.

THE heavens declare the glory of God; and the firmament sheweth his handywork.

✣ Day unto day uttereth speech, and night unto night sheweth knowledge.

There is no speech nor language, *where* their voice is not heard.

✣ Their line is gone out through all the earth, and their words to the ends of the world.

In them hath he set a tabernacle for the sun. Which *is* as a bridegroom coming out of his chamber, *and* rejoiceth as a strong man to run a race.

✣ His going forth *is* from the end of the heaven, and his circuit unto the ends of it: and there is nothing hid from the heat thereof.

The law of the LORD *is* perfect, converting the soul: the testimony of the LORD *is* sure, making wise the simple.

✠ The statutes of the LORD *are* right, rejoicing the heart: the commandment of the LORD *is* pure, enlightening the eyes.

The fear of the LORD *is* clean, enduring for ever: the judgments of the LORD *are* true *and* righteous altogether.

✠ More to be desired *are they* than gold, yea, than much fine gold: sweeter also than honey and the honeycomb.

Moreover, by them is thy servant warned: *and* in keeping of them *there is* great reward.

✠ Who can understand *his* errors? cleanse thou me from secret *faults*.

Keep back thy servant also from presumptuous *sins;* let them not have dominion over me: then shall I be upright, and I shall be innocent from the great transgression.

✠ Let the words of my mouth, and the meditations of my heart, be acceptable in thy sight, O LORD, my strength, and my redeemer.

Psalm xix. 1–14.

Eighteenth Selection.

Verity and Judgment are His Works.

PRAISE ye the Lord.
✙ I will praise the Lord with *my* whole heart, in the assembly of the upright, and *in* the congregation.

The works of the Lord *are* great, sought out of all them that have pleasure therein.

✙ His work *is* honourable and glorious: and his righteousness endureth for ever.

He hath made his wonderful works to be remembered: the Lord *is* gracious and full of compassion.

✙ He hath given meat unto them that fear him: he will ever be mindful of his covenant.

He hath shewed his people the power of his works, that he may give them the heritage of the heathen.

✙ The works of his hands *are* verity and judgment; all his commandments *are* sure.

They stand fast for ever and ever, *and are* done in truth and uprightness.

✙ He sent redemption unto his people:

he hath commanded his covenant for ever: holy and reverend *is* his name.

The fear of the LORD *is* the beginning of wisdom : a good understanding have all they that do *his commandments :* his praise endureth for ever.

Psalm cxi. 1-10.

Nineteenth Selection.

His Name is Holy.

THE LORD reigneth; let the people tremble :

✚ He sitteth *between* the cherubim ; let the earth be moved.

The LORD *is* great in Zion ; and he *is* high above all the people.

✚ Let them praise thy great and terrible name ; *for* it *is* holy.

The king's strength also loveth judgment; thou dost establish equity, thou executest judgment and righteousness in Jacob.

✚ Exalt ye the LORD our God, and worship at his footstool ; *for* he *is* holy.

Moses and Aaron among his priests, and Samuel among them that call upon his name; they called upon the LORD, and he answered them.

✠ He spake unto them in the cloudy pillar: they kept his testimonies, and the ordinance *that* he gave them.

Thou answeredst them, O LORD our God: thou wast a God that forgavest them, though thou tookest vengeance of their inventions.

✠ Exalt the LORD our God, and worship at his holy hill; for the LORD our God *is* holy.

Psalm xcix. 1–9.

Twentieth Selection.

Thy Judgments are Good.

TEACH me, O LORD, the way of thy statutes; and I shall keep it *unto* the end.

✠ Give me understanding, and I shall keep thy law; yea, I shall observe it with *my* whole heart.

Make me to go in the path of thy commandments; for therein do I delight.

✠ Incline my heart unto thy testimonies, and not to covetousness.

Turn away mine eyes from beholding vanity; *and* quicken thou me in thy way.

✠ Establish thy word unto thy servant, who *is devoted* to thy fear.

Turn away my reproach which I fear: for thy judgments *are* good.

✠ Behold, I have longed after thy precepts: quicken me in thy righteousness.

Let thy mercies come also unto me, O LORD, *even* thy salvation, according to thy word.

✠ So shall I have wherewith to answer him that reproacheth me: for I trust in thy word.

And take not the word of truth utterly out of my mouth; for I have hoped in thy judgments.

✠ So shall I keep thy law continually for ever and ever.

And I will walk at liberty: for I seek thy precepts.

✠ I will speak of thy testimonies also before kings, and will not be ashamed.

And I will delight myself in thy commandments, which I have loved.

✠ My hands also will I lift up unto thy commandments, which I have loved; and I will meditate in thy statutes.

Psalm cxix. 33-48.

V.

OF GOD'S GOODNESS.

Twenty-first Selection.

For He is Good.

O GIVE thanks unto the Lord, for *he is good*: for his mercy *endureth* for ever.

✣ Let the redeemed of the Lord say *so*, whom he hath redeemed from the hand of the enemy;

And gathered them out of the lands, from the east, and from the west, from the north, and from the south.

✣ They wandered in the wilderness in a solitary way; they found no city to dwell in.

Hungry and thirsty, their soul fainted in them.

✣ Then they cried unto the Lord in their trouble, *and* he delivered them out of their distresses.

And he led them forth by the right way, that they might go to a city of habitation.

✠ Oh that *men* would praise the Lord *for* his goodness, and *for* his wonderful works to the children of men!

For he satisfieth the longing soul, and filleth the hungry soul with goodness.

✠ Such as sit in darkness and in the shadow of death, *being* bound in affliction and iron;

Because they rebelled against the words of God, and contemned the counsel of the Most High:

✠ Therefore he brought down their heart with labour; they fell down, and *there was* none to help.

Then they cried unto the Lord in their trouble, *and* he saved them out of their distresses.

✠ He brought them out of darkness and the shadow of death, and brake their bands in sunder.

Oh that *men* would praise the Lord *for* his goodness, and *for* his wonderful works to the children of men!

Psalm cvii. 1–15.

Twenty-second Selection.

The Loving-kindness of the Lord.

OH that *men* would praise the LORD *for* his goodness, and *for* his wonderful works to the children of men!

✣ Let them exalt him also in the congregation of the people, and praise him in the assembly of the elders.

He turneth rivers into a wilderness, and the water-springs into dry ground;

✣ A fruitful land into barrenness, for the wickedness of them that dwell therein.

He turneth the wilderness into a standing water, and dry ground into water-springs.

✣ And there he maketh the hungry to dwell, that they may prepare a city for habitation;

And sow the fields, and plant vineyards, which may yield fruits of increase.

✣ He blesseth them also, so that they are multiplied greatly; and suffereth not their cattle to decrease.

Again, they are minished and brought low through oppression, affliction, and sorrow.

§ 23 *Of God's Goodness.* 35

✣ He poureth contempt upon princes, and causeth them to wander in the wilderness, *where there is* no way.

Yet setteth he the poor on high from affliction, and maketh *him* families like a flock.

✣ The righteous shall see *it*, and rejoice: and all iniquity shall stop her mouth.

Whoso *is* wise, and will observe these *things*, even they shall understand the loving-kindness of the Lord.

Psalm cvii. 31–43.

Twenty-third Selection.

Every Day Will I Bless Thee.

I WILL extol thee, my God, O King; and I will bless thy name for ever and ever.

✣ Every day will I bless thee; and I will praise thy name for ever and ever.

Great *is* the Lord, and greatly to be praised; and his greatness *is* unsearchable.

✣ One generation shall praise thy works to another, and shall declare thy mighty acts.

I will speak of the glorious honour of thy majesty, and of thy wondrous works.

✠ And *men* shall speak of the might of thy terrible acts: and I will declare thy greatness.

They shall abundantly utter the memory of thy great goodness, and shall sing of thy righteousness.

✠ The LORD *is* gracious, and full of compassion; slow to anger, and of great mercy.

The LORD *is* good to all: and his tender mercies *are* over all his works.

✠ All thy works shall praise thee, O LORD; and thy saints shall bless thee.

They shall speak of the glory of thy kingdom, and talk of thy power;

✠ To make known to the sons of men his mighty acts, and the glorious majesty of his kingdom.

Thy kingdom *is* an everlasting kingdom, and thy dominion *endureth* throughout all generations.

✠ The LORD upholdeth all that fall, and raiseth up all *those that be* bowed down.

The eyes of all wait upon thee; and thou givest them their meat in due season.

✠ Thou openest thy hand, and satisfiest the desire of every living thing.

The LORD *is* righteous in all his ways, and holy in all his works.

✠ The LORD *is* nigh unto all them that call upon him, to all that call upon him in truth.

He will fulfil the desire of them that fear him: he also will hear their cry, and will save them.

✠ The LORD preserveth all them that love him: but all the wicked will he destroy.

My mouth shall speak the praise of the LORD: and let all flesh bless his holy name for ever and ever.

Psalm cxlv. 1-21.

Twenty-fourth Selection.

Chastisement and Deliverance.

PRAISE ye the LORD. O give thanks unto the LORD; for *he is* good: for his mercy *endureth* for ever.

✠ Who can utter the mighty acts of the LORD? *who* can shew forth all his praise?

Blessed *are* they that keep judgment, *and* he that doeth righteousness at all times.

✠ Remember me, O Lord, with the favour *that thou bearest unto* thy people: O visit me with thy salvation;

That I may see the good of thy chosen, that I may rejoice in the gladness of thy nation, that I may glory with thine inheritance.

✠ We have sinned with our fathers, we have committed iniquity, we have done wickedly.

Our fathers understood not thy wonders in Egypt; they remembered not the multitude of thy mercies; but provoked *him* at the sea, *even* at the Red sea.

✠ Nevertheless he saved them for his name's sake, that he might make his mighty power to be known.

Many times did he deliver them; but they provoked *him* with their counsel; and were brought low for their iniquity.

✠ Nevertheless he regarded their affliction, when he heard their cry:

And he remembered for them his covenant, and repented according to the multitude of his mercies.

✠ He made them also to be pitied of all those that carried them captives.

Save us, O LORD our God, and gather us from among the heathen, to give thanks unto thy holy name, *and* to triumph in thy praise.

✠ Blessed *be* the LORD God of Israel from everlasting to everlasting: and let all the people say, Amen. Praise ye the LORD.

Psalm cvi. 1-8, 43-48.

Twenty-fifth Selection.

God's Wonders in the Deep.

OH that *men* would praise the LORD *for* his goodness, and *for* his wonderful works to the children of men!

✠ And let them sacrifice the sacrifices of thanksgiving, and declare his works with rejoicing.

They that go down to the sea in ships, that do business in great waters;

✠ These see the works of the LORD, and his wonders in the deep.

For he commandeth, and raiseth the

stormy wind, which lifteth up the waves thereof.

✠ They mount up to the heaven, they go down again to the depths: their soul is melted because of trouble.

They reel to and fro, and stagger like a drunken man, and are at their wit's end.

✠ Then they cry unto the LORD in their trouble, and he bringeth them out of their distresses.

He maketh the storm a calm, so that the waves thereof are still.

✠ Then are they glad because they be quiet; so he bringeth them unto their desired haven.

Oh that *men* would praise the LORD *for* his goodness, and *for* his wonderful works to the children of men!

Psalm cvii. 21–31.

Twenty-sixth Selection.

Thou Visitest the Earth.

PRAISE waiteth for thee, O God, in Zion: and unto thee shall the vow be performed.

✟ O thou that hearest prayer, unto thee shall all flesh come.

Iniquities prevail against me: *as for* our transgressions, thou shalt purge them away.

✟ Blessed *is the man whom* thou choosest, and causest to approach *unto thee, that* he may dwell in thy courts:

We shall be satisfied with the goodness of thy house, *even* of thy holy temple.

✟ *By* terrible things in righteousness wilt thou answer us, O God of our Salvation;

Who art the confidence of all the ends of the earth, and of them that are afar off *upon* the sea:

✟ Which by his strength setteth fast the mountains; *being* girded with power:

Which stilleth the noise of the seas, the noise of their waves, and the tumult of the people.

✟ They also that dwell in the uttermost parts are afraid at thy tokens: thou makest the outgoings of the morning and evening to rejoice.

Thou visitest the earth, and waterest it: thou greatly enrichest it with the river of God, *which* is full of water: thou preparest them corn, when thou hast so provided for it.

✝ Thou waterest the ridges thereof abundantly: thou settlest the furrows thereof:

Thou makest it soft with showers: thou blessest the springing thereof.

✝ Thou crownest the year with thy goodness; and thy paths drop fatness.

They drop *upon* the pastures of the wilderness: and the little hills rejoice on every side.

✝ The pastures are clothed with flocks; the valleys also are covered over with corn: they shout for joy; they also sing.

Psalm lxv. 1–13.

Twenty-seventh Selection.

National Blessings.

O GIVE thanks unto the LORD; call upon his name: make known his deeds among the people.

✝ Sing unto him, sing psalms unto him: talk ye of all his wondrous works.

Glory ye in his holy name: let the heart of them rejoice that seek the LORD.

✝ Seek the LORD, and his strength: seek his face evermore.

§ 28   *Of God's Goodness.*   43

Remember his marvellous works that he hath done; his wonders, and the judgments of his mouth;

✠ O ye seed of Abraham his servant, ye children of Jacob his chosen.

He *is* the Lord our God: his judgments *are* in all the earth.

✠ He hath remembered his covenant for ever, the word *which* he commanded to a thousand generations.

And he brought forth his people with joy, *and* his chosen with gladness:

✠ And gave them the lands of the heathen: and they inherited the labour of the people;

That they might observe his statutes, and keeps his laws.   Praise ye the Lord.
Psalm cv. 1–8, 43–45.

Twenty-eighth Selection.

O Give Thanks.

O GIVE thanks unto the Lord; for *he is* good: for his mercy *endureth* for ever.

✠ O give thanks unto the God of gods: for his mercy *endureth* for ever.

O give thanks to the Lord of lords: for his mercy *endureth* for ever.

✠ To him who alone doeth great wonders: for his mercy *endureth* for ever.

To him that by wisdom made the heavens: for his mercy *endureth* for ever.

✠ To him that stretched out the earth above the waters: for his mercy *endureth* for ever.

To him that made great lights: for his mercy *endureth* for ever:

✠ The sun to rule by day: for his mercy *endureth* for ever:

The moon and stars to rule by night: for his mercy *endureth* for ever.

✠ To him that smote Egypt in their first-born: for his mercy *endureth* for ever:

And brought out Israel from among them: for his mercy *endureth* for ever:

✠ With a strong hand, and with a stretched out arm: for his mercy *endureth* for ever.

To him which divided the Red sea into parts: for his mercy *endureth* for ever:

✠ And made Israel to pass through the midst of it: for his mercy *endureth* for ever:

But overthrew Pharaoh and his host in the Red sea: for his mercy *endureth* for ever.

✠ To him which led his people through the wilderness: for his mercy *endureth* for ever.

To him which smote great kings: for his mercy *endureth* for ever:

✠ And slew famous kings: for his mercy *endureth* for ever:

Sihon king of the Amorites: for his mercy *endureth* for ever:

✠ And Og the king of Bashan: for his mercy *endureth* for ever:

And gave their land for a heritage: for his mercy *endureth* for ever:

✠ *Even* a heritage unto Israel his servant: for his mercy *endureth* for ever.

Who remembered us in our low estate: for his mercy *endureth* for ever:

✠ And hath redeemed us from our enemies: for his mercy *endureth* for ever.

Who giveth food to all flesh: for his mercy *endureth* for ever.

✠ O give thanks unto the God of heaven: for his mercy *endureth* for ever.

Psalm cxxxvi. 1–26.

VI.

OF GOD'S MERCY.

Twenty-ninth Selection.

His Mercy Endureth Forever.

O GIVE thanks unto the LORD; for *he is* good: because his mercy *endureth* for ever.

✠ Let Israel now say, that his mercy *endureth* for ever.

Let the house of Aaron now say, that his mercy *endureth* for ever.

✠ Let them now that fear the LORD say, that his mercy *endureth* for ever.

I called upon the LORD in distress: the LORD answered me, *and set me* in a large place.

✠ The LORD *is* on my side; I will not fear: what can man do unto me?

Open to me the gates of righteousness: I will go into them, *and* I will praise the LORD:

✠ This gate of the LORD, into which the righteous shall enter.

I will praise thee: for thou hast heard me, and art become my salvation.

✠ The stone *which* the builders refused is become the head *stone* of the corner.

This is the Lord's doing; it *is* marvellous in our eyes.

✠ This *is* the day *which* the Lord hath made; we will rejoice and be glad in it.

Save now, I beseech thee, O Lord: O Lord, I beseech thee, send now prosperity.

✠ Blessed *be* he that cometh in the name of the Lord:

We have blessed you out of the house of the Lord.

Psalm cxviii. 1-6, 19-26.

Thirtieth Selection.

Forget Not All His Benefits.

BLESS the Lord, O my soul: and all that is within me, *bless* his holy name.

✠ Bless the Lord, O my soul, and forget not all his benefits:

Who forgiveth all thine iniquities; who healeth all thy diseases;

✠ Who redeemeth thy life from destruction; who crowneth thee with loving-kindness and tender mercies;

Who satisfieth thy mouth with good *things; so that* thy youth is renewed like the eagle's.

✠ The Lord executeth righteousness and judgment for all that are oppressed.

He made known his ways unto Moses, his acts unto the children of Israel.

✠ The Lord *is* merciful and gracious, slow to anger, and plenteous in mercy.

He will not always chide: neither will he keep *his anger* for ever.

✠ He hath not dealt with us after our sins; nor rewarded us according to our iniquities.

For as the heaven is high above the earth, *so* great is his mercy toward them that fear him.

✠ As far as the east is from the west, *so* far hath he removed our transgressions from us.

Like as a father pitieth *his* children, *so* the Lord pitieth them that fear him.

✠ For he knoweth our frame; he remembereth that we *are* dust.

As for man, his days *are* as grass: as a flower of the field, so he flourisheth.

✠ For the wind passeth over it, and it is gone; and the place thereof shall know it no more.

But the mercy of the LORD *is* from everlasting to everlasting upon them that fear him, and his righteousness unto children's children;

✠ To such as keep his covenant, and to those that remember his commandments to do them.

The LORD hath prepared his throne in the heavens; and his kingdom ruleth over all.

✠ Bless the LORD, ye his angels, that excel in strength, that do his commandments, hearkening unto the voice of his word.

Bless ye the LORD, all *ye* his hosts; *ye* ministers of his, that do his pleasure.

✠ Bless the LORD, all his works in all places of his dominion: bless the LORD, O my soul.

Psalm ciii. 1–22.

Thirty-first Selection.

How Excellent is Thy Loving-kindness.

THY mercy, O Lord, *is* in the heavens; and thy faithfulness *reacheth* unto the clouds.

✠ Thy righteousness *is* like the great mountains; thy judgments *are* a great deep:

O Lord, thou preservest man and beast.

✠ How excellent *is* thy loving-kindness, O God! therefore the children of men put their trust under the shadow of thy wings.

They shall be abundantly satisfied with the fatness of thy house;

✠ And thou shalt make them drink of the river of thy pleasures.

For with thee *is* the fountain of life: in thy light shall we see light.

✠ O continue thy loving-kindness unto them that know thee;

And thy righteousness to the upright in heart.

Psalm xxxvi. 5–10.

Thirty-second Selection.

The Giver of the Heart's Desire.

THE king shall joy in thy strength, O Lord; and in thy salvation how greatly shall he rejoice!

✠ Thou hast given him his heart's desire, and hast not withholden the request of his lips.

For thou preventest him with the blessings of goodness: thou settest a crown of pure gold on his head.

✠ He asked life of thee, *and* thou gavest *it* him, *even* length of days for ever and ever.

His glory *is* great in thy salvation: honour and majesty hast thou laid upon him.

✠ For thou hast made him most blessed for ever: thou hast made him exceeding glad with thy countenance.

For the king trusteth in the Lord, and through the mercy of the Most High he shall not be moved.

✠ Be thou exalted, Lord, in thine own strength: *so* will we sing and praise thy power.

Psalm xxi. 1–7, 13.

Thirty-third Selection.

The Lord hath Respect unto the Lowly.

I WILL praise thee with my whole heart:
✟ Before the gods will I sing praise unto thee.

I will worship toward thy holy temple, and praise thy name for thy loving-kindness and for thy truth: for thou hast magnified thy word above all thy name.

✟ In the day when I cried thou answeredst me, *and* strengthenedst me *with* strength in my soul.

All the kings of the earth shall praise thee, O LORD, when they hear the words of thy mouth.

✟ Yea, they shall sing in the ways of the LORD: for great *is* the glory of the LORD.

Though the LORD *be* high, yet hath he respect unto the lowly: but the proud he knoweth afar off.

✟ Though I walk in the midst of trouble, thou wilt revive me:

Thou shalt stretch forth thy hand against the wrath of mine enemies, and thy right hand shall save me.

✠ The LORD will perfect *that which* concerneth me: thy mercy, O LORD, *endureth* for ever: forsake not the works of thine own hands.

Psalm cxxxviii. 1–8.

Thirty-fourth Selection.

Thou Tellest My Wanderings.

BE merciful unto me, O God: for man would swallow me up; he fighting daily oppresseth me.

✠ Mine enemies would daily swallow *me* up: for *they be* many that fight against me, O thou Most High.

What time I am afraid, I will trust in thee.

✠ In God I will praise his word, in God I have put my trust; I will not fear what flesh can do unto me.

Every day they wrest my words: all their thoughts *are* against me for evil.

✠ They gather themselves together, they hide themselves, they mark my steps, when they wait for my soul.

Shall they escape by iniquity? in *thine* anger cast down the people, O God.

✧ Thou tellest my wanderings : put thou my tears into thy bottle : *are they* not in thy book ?

When I cry *unto thee*, then shall mine enemies turn back : this I know ; for God *is* for me.

✧ In God will I praise *his* word : in the LORD will I praise *his* word.

In God have I put my trust : I will not be afraid what man can do unto me.

✧ Thy vows *are* upon me, O God : I will render praises unto thee.

For thou hast delivered my soul from death : *wilt* not *thou deliver* my feet from falling, that I may walk before God in the light of the living ?

Psalm lvi. 1–13.

Thirty-fifth Selection.

Verily God hath Heard Me.

MAKE a joyful noise unto God, all ye lands :

✧ Sing forth the honour of his name : make his praise glorious.

Say unto God, How terrible *art thou in* thy works ! through the greatness of thy power shall thine enemies submit themselves unto thee.

✢ All the earth shall worship thee, and shall sing unto thee; they shall sing *to* thy name.

Come and see the works of God: *he is* terrible *in his* doing toward the children of men.

✢ He turned the sea into dry *land:* they went through the flood on foot: there did we rejoice in him.

He ruleth by his power for ever;

✢ His eyes behold the nations: let not the rebellious exalt themselves.

O bless our God, ye people, and make the voice of his praise to be heard:

✢ Which holdeth our soul in life, and suffereth not our feet to be moved.

Come *and* hear, all ye that fear God, and I will declare what he hath done for my soul.

✢ I cried unto him with my mouth, and he was extolled with my tongue.

If I regard iniquity in my heart, the Lord will not hear *me:*

✢ *But* verily God hath heard *me;* he hath attended to the voice of my prayer.

Blessed *be* God, which hath not turned away my prayer, nor his mercy from me.

Psalm lxvi. 1–9, 16–20.

Thirty-sixth Selection.

I Love the Lord.

I LOVE the LORD, because he hath heard my voice *and* my supplications.

✠ Because he hath inclined his ear unto me, therefore will I call upon *him* as long as I live.

The sorrows of death compassed me, and the pains of hell gat hold upon me: I found trouble and sorrow.

✠ Then called I upon the name of the LORD; O LORD, I beseech thee, deliver my soul.

Gracious *is* the LORD, and righteous; yea, our God *is* merciful.

✠ The LORD preserveth the simple: I was brought low, and he helped me.

Return unto thy rest, O my soul; for the LORD hath dealt bountifully with thee.

✠ For thou hast delivered my soul from

death, mine eyes from tears, *and* my feet from falling.

I will walk before the LORD in the land of the living.

✜ I believed, therefore have I spoken: I was greatly afflicted: I said in my haste, All men *are* liars.

What shall I render unto the LORD *for* all his benefits toward me?

✜ I will take the cup of salvation, and call upon the name of the LORD.

I will pay my vows unto the LORD now in the presence of all his people.

✜ Precious in the sight of the LORD *is* the death of his saints.

O LORD, truly I *am* thy servant; I *am* thy servant, *and* the son of thine handmaid: thou hast loosed my bonds.

✜ I will offer to thee the sacrifice of thanksgiving, and will call upon the name of the LORD.

I will pay my vows unto the LORD now in the presence of all his people.

✜ In the courts of the LORD'S house, in the midst of thee, O Jerusalem.

Praise ye the LORD.

Psalm cxvi. 1-19.

Thirty-seventh Selection.

In the Shadow of Thy Wings.

BE merciful unto me, O God, be merciful unto me: for my soul trusteth in thee: yea, in the shadow of thy wings will I make my refuge, until *these* calamities be overpast.

✠ I will cry unto God Most High; unto God that performeth *all things* for me.

He shall send from heaven, and save me *from* the reproach of him that would swallow me up.

✠ God shall send forth his mercy and his truth.

My soul *is* among lions: *and* I lie *even among* them that are set on fire, *even* the sons of men, whose teeth *are* spears and arrows, and their tongue a sharp sword.

✠ Be thou exalted, O God, above the heavens; *let* thy glory *be* above all the earth.

They have prepared a net for my steps; my soul is bowed down: they have digged a pit before me, into the midst whereof they are fallen *themselves*.

✠ My heart is fixed, O God, my heart is fixed : I will sing and give praise.

Awake up, my glory; awake psaltery and harp : I *myself* will awake early.

✠ I will praise thee, O Lord, among the people : I will sing unto thee among the nations.

For thy mercy *is* great unto the heavens, and thy truth unto the clouds.

✠ Be thou exalted, O God, above the heavens : *let* thy glory *be* above all the earth.

Psalm lvii. 1–11.

Thirty-eighth Selection.

The Great Helper.

PRAISE ye the Lord.

✠ Praise the Lord, O my soul.

While I live I will praise the Lord : I will sing praises unto my God while I have any being.

✠ Put not your trust in princes, *nor* in the son of man, in whom *there is* no help.

His breath goeth forth, he returneth to his earth; in that very day his thoughts perish.

✠ Happy *is he* that *hath* the God of Jacob for his help, whose hope *is* in the Lord his God:

Which made heaven, and earth, the sea, and all that therein *is:* which keepeth truth for ever:

✠ Which executeth judgment for the oppressed; which giveth food to the hungry.

The Lord looseth the prisoners: the Lord openeth *the eyes of* the blind:

✠ The Lord raiseth them that are bowed down: the Lord loveth the righteous:

The Lord preserveth the strangers; he relieveth the fatherless and widow: but the way of the wicked he turneth upside down.

✠ The Lord shall reign for ever, *even* thy God, O Zion, unto all generations. Praise ye the Lord.

Psalm cxlvi. 1–10.

Thirty-ninth Selection.

This Poor Man Cried.

I WILL bless the Lord at all times: his praise *shall* continually *be* in my mouth.

✣ My soul shall make her boast in the Lord: the humble shall hear *thereof*, and be glad.

O magnify the Lord with me, and let us exalt his name together.

✣ I sought the Lord, and he heard me, and delivered me from all my fears.

They looked unto him, and were lightened: and their faces were not ashamed.

✣ This poor man cried, and the Lord heard *him*, and saved him out of all his troubles.

The angel of the Lord encampeth round about them that fear him, and delivereth them.

✣ O taste and see that the Lord *is* good: blessed *is* the man *that* trusteth in him.

O fear the Lord, ye his saints; for *there is* no want to them that fear him.

✣ The young lions do lack, and suffer hunger: but they that seek the Lord shall not want any good *thing*.

Come, ye children, hearken unto me: I will teach you the fear of the Lord.

✣ What man *is he that* desireth life, *and* loveth *many* days, that he may see good?

Keep thy tongue from evil, and thy lips from speaking guile.

✠ Depart from evil, and do good; seek peace, and pursue it.

The eyes of the LORD *are* upon the righteous, and his ears *are open* unto their cry.

✠ The face of the LORD *is* against them that do evil, to cut off the remembrance of them from the earth.

The *righteous* cry, and the LORD heareth, and delivereth them out of all their troubles.

✠ The LORD *is* nigh unto them that are of a broken heart; and saveth such as be of a contrite spirit.

Many *are* the afflictions of the righteous: but the LORD delivereth him out of them all.

✠ He keepeth all his bones: not one of them is broken.

Evil shall slay the wicked: and they that hate the righteous shall be desolate.

✠ The LORD redeemeth the soul of his servants: and none of them that trust in him shall be desolate.

Psalm xxxiv. 1–22.

VII.

OF GOD'S FAITHFULNESS.

Fortieth Selection.

The Covenant.

I WILL sing of the mercies of the LORD for ever:

✢ With my mouth will I make known thy faithfulness to all generations.

For I have said, Mercy shall be built up for ever:

✢ Thy faithfulness shalt thou establish in the very heavens.

I have made a covenant with my chosen, I have sworn unto David my servant,

✢ Thy seed will I establish for ever, and build up thy throne to all generations.

And the heavens shall praise thy wonders, O LORD: thy faithfulness also in the congregation of the saints.

✢ For who in the heaven can be compared unto the LORD? *who* among the sons of the mighty can be likened unto the LORD?

God is greatly to be feared in the assembly of the saints, and to be had in reverence of all *them that are* about him.

Psalm lxxxix. 1–7.

Forty-first Selection.

Remember the Days of Old.

GIVE ear, O ye heavens, and I will speak;

✠ And hear, O earth, the words of my mouth.

My doctrine shall drop as the rain, my speech shall distil as the dew, as the small rain upon the tender herb, and as the showers upon the grass:

✠ Because I will publish the name of the LORD: ascribe ye greatness unto our God.

He is the Rock, his word *is* perfect: for all his ways *are* judgment:

✠ A God of truth and without iniquity, just and right *is* he.

They have corrupted themselves, their spot *is* not *the spot* of his children:

✠ *They are* a perverse and crooked generation.

Do ye thus requite the LORD, O foolish people and unwise? *is* not he thy father *that* hath bought thee?

✢ Hath he not made thee, and established thee?

Remember the days of old, consider the years of many generations:

✢ Ask thy father, and he will shew thee; thy elders, and they will tell thee.

When the Most High divided to their nations their inheritance, when he separated the sons of Adam, he set the bounds of the people according to the number of the children of Israel.

✢ For the LORD's portion *is* his people; Jacob *is* the lot of his inheritance.

He found him in a desert land, and in the waste howling wilderness;

✢ He led him about, he instructed him, he kept him as the apple of his eye.

As an eagle stirreth up her nest, fluttereth over her young, spreadeth abroad her wings, taketh them, beareth them on her wings:

✢ *So* the LORD alone did lead him, and *there was* no strange god with him.

Deuteronomy xxxii. 1–12.

Forty-second Selection.

The Lord is Our Defence.

O LORD God of hosts, who *is* a strong LORD like unto thee? or to thy faithfulness round about thee?

✠ Thou rulest the raging of the sea: when the waves thereof arise, thou stillest them.

Thou hast broken Rahab in pieces, as one that is slain; thou hast scattered thine enemies with thy strong arm.

✠ The heavens *are* thine, the earth also *is* thine: *as for* the world, and the fulness thereof, thou hast founded them.

The north and the south thou hast created them: Tabor and Hermon shall rejoice in thy name.

✠ Thou hast a mighty arm: strong is thy hand, *and* high is thy right hand.

Justice and judgment *are* the habitation of thy throne: mercy and truth shall go before thy face.

✠ Blessed *is* the people that know the joyful sound: they shall walk, O LORD, in the light of thy countenance.

§ 43   *Of God's Faithfulness.*   67

In thy name shall they rejoice all the day : and in thy righteousness shall they be exalted.

✠ For thou *art* the glory of their strength; and in thy favour our horn shall be exalted.

For the LORD *is* our defence; and the Holy One of Israel *is* our King.

Psalm lxxxix. 8–18.

Forty-third Selection.

The People of His Pasture.

O COME, let us sing unto the LORD :
✠ Let us make a joyful noise to the Rock of our salvation.

Let us come before his presence with thanksgiving, and make a joyful noise unto him with psalms.

✠ For the LORD *is* a great God, and a great King above all gods.

In his hand *are* the deep places of the earth : the strength of the hills *is* his also.

✠ The sea *is* his, and he made it : and his hands formed the dry *land*.

O come, let us worship and bow down : let us kneel before the LORD our maker.

✠ For he *is* our God; and we *are* the people of his pasture, and the sheep of his hand.

To-day, if ye will hear his voice, harden not your heart, as in the provocation, *and* as *in* the day of temptation in the wilderness:

✠ When your fathers tempted me, proved me, and saw my work.

Forty years long was I grieved with *this* generation, and said, It *is* a people that do err in their heart, and they have not known my ways:

✠ Unto whom I sware in my wrath, that they should not enter into my rest.

Psalm xcv. 1-11.

Forty-fourth Selection.

I will Declare Thy Name.

I WILL declare thy name unto my brethren: in the midst of the congregation will I praise thee.

✠ Ye that fear the LORD, praise him; all ye the seed of Jacob, glorify him; and fear him, all ye the seed of Israel.

§ 44   *Of God's Faithfulness.*

For he hath not despised nor abhorred the affliction of the afflicted; neither hath he hid his face from him; but when he cried unto him, he heard.

✠ My praise *shall be* of thee in the great congregation: I will pay my vows before them that fear him.

The meek shall eat and be satisfied: they shall praise the Lord that seek him: your heart shall live for ever.

✠ All the ends of the world shall remember and turn unto the Lord:

And all the kindreds of the nations shall worship before thee.

✠ For the kingdom *is* the Lord's: and he *is* the governor among the nations.

All *they that be* fat upon earth shall eat and worship: all they that go down to the dust shall bow before him: and none can keep alive his own soul.

✠ A seed shall serve him; it shall be accounted to the Lord for a generation.

They shall come, and shall declare his righteousness unto a people that shall be born, that he hath done *this*.

Psalm xxii. 22–31.

Forty-fifth Selection.

Blessed is the Nation.

REJOICE in the Lord, O ye righteous: *for* praise is comely for the upright.

✠ Praise the Lord with harp: sing unto him with the psaltery *and* an instrument of ten strings.

Sing unto him a new song; play skilfully with a loud noise.

✠ For the word of the Lord *is* right; and all his works *are done* in truth.

He loveth righteousness and judgment: the earth is full of the goodness of the Lord.

✠ By the word of the Lord were the heavens made; and all the host of them by the breath of his mouth.

He gathereth the waters of the sea together as a heap: he layeth up the depth in storehouses.

✠ Let all the earth fear the Lord: let all the inhabitants of the world stand in awe of him.

For he spake, and it was *done;* he commanded, and it stood fast.

✤ The Lord bringeth the counsel of the heathen to nought: he maketh the devices of the people of none effect.

The counsel of the Lord standeth for ever, the thoughts of his heart to all generations.

✤ Blessed *is* the nation whose God *is* the Lord; *and* the people *whom* he hath chosen for his own inheritance.

Psalm xxxiii. 1-12.

Forty-sixth Selection.

We have Waited for Him.

O LORD, thou *art* my God; I will exalt thee, I will praise thy name; for thou hast done wonderful *things*.

✤ *Thy* counsels of old *are* faithfulness *and* truth.

For thou hast made of a city a heap; *of* a defenced city a ruin: a palace of strangers to be no city; it shall never be built.

✤ Therefore shall the strong people glorify thee, the city of the terrible nations shall fear thee.

For thou hast been a strength to the poor, a strength to the needy in his distress, a refuge from the storm, a shadow from the heat, when the blast of the terrible ones *is* as a storm *against* the wall.

✞ Thou shalt bring down the noise of strangers, as the heat in a dry place; *even* the heat with the shadow of a cloud: the branch of the terrible ones shall be brought low.

And in this mountain shall the Lord of hosts make unto all people a feast of fat things, a feast of wines on the lees, of fat things full of marrow, of wines on the lees well refined.

✞ And he will destroy in this mountain the face of the covering cast over all people, and the vail that is spread over all nations.

He will swallow up death in victory; and the Lord God will wipe away tears from off all faces;

✞ And the rebuke of his people shall he take away from off all the earth: for the Lord hath spoken *it*.

And it shall be said in that day, Lo, this *is* our God; we have waited for him, and he will save us:

§ 47   *Of God's Faithfulness.*   73

✠ This *is* the Lord; we have waited for him, we will be glad and rejoice in his salvation.

Isaiah xxv. 1-9.

Forty-seventh Selection.

He hath not Dealt so with Any Nation.

PRAISE ye the Lord:
✠ For *it is* good to sing praises unto our God; for *it is* pleasant; *and* praise is comely.

The Lord doth build up Jerusalem: he gathereth together the outcasts of Israel.

✠ He healeth the broken in heart, and bindeth up their wounds.

He telleth the number of the stars; he calleth them all by *their* names.

✠ Great *is* our Lord, and of great power: his understanding *is* infinite.

The Lord lifteth up the meek: he casteth the wicked down to the ground.

✠ Sing unto the Lord with thanksgiving; sing praise upon the harp unto our God:

Who covereth the heaven with clouds, who prepareth rain for the earth, who maketh grass to grow upon the mountains.

✠ He giveth to the beast his food, *and* to the young ravens which cry.

He delighteth not in the strength of the horse: he taketh not pleasure in the legs of a man.

✠ The LORD taketh pleasure in them that fear him, in those that hope in his mercy.

Praise the LORD, O Jerusalem; praise thy God, O Zion.

✠ For he hath strengthened the bars of thy gates; he hath blessed thy children within thee:

He maketh peace *in* thy borders, *and* filleth thee with the finest of the wheat.

✠ He sendeth forth his commandment *upon* earth: his word runneth very swiftly.

He giveth snow like wool: he scattereth the hoar-frost like ashes.

✠ He casteth forth his ice like morsels: who can stand before his cold?

He sendeth out his word, and melteth them: he causeth his wind to blow, *and* the waters flow.

✠ He sheweth his word unto Jacob, his statutes and his judgments unto Israel.

He hath not dealt so with any nation: and *as for his* judgments, they have not known them.

✠ Praise ye the LORD.   *Psalm* cxlvii. 1-20.

Forty-eighth Selection.

A Morning Prayer.

GIVE ear to my words, O LORD, consider my meditation.

✠ Hearken unto the voice of my cry, my King, and my God: for unto thee will I pray.

My voice shalt thou hear in the morning, O LORD; in the morning will I direct *my prayer* unto thee, and will look up.

✠ For thou *art* not a God that hath pleasure in wickedness: neither shall evil dwell with thee.

The foolish shall not stand in thy sight: thou hatest all workers of iniquity.

✠ Thou shalt destroy them that speak leasing: the LORD will abhor the bloody and deceitful man.

But as for me, I will come *into* thy house in the multitude of thy mercy: *and* in thy fear will I worship toward thy holy temple.

✠ Lead me, O Lord, in thy righteousness, because of mine enemies; make thy way straight before my face.

But let all those that put their trust in thee rejoice: let them ever shout for joy, because thou defendest them: let them also that love thy name be joyful in thee.

✠ For thou, Lord, wilt bless the righteous; with favour wilt thou compass him as *with* a shield.

Psalm v. 1-8, 11-12.

Forty-ninth Selection.

Serve the Lord with Gladness.

MAKE a joyful noise unto the Lord, all ye lands.

✠ Serve the Lord with gladness: come before his presence with singing.

Know ye that the Lord he *is* God: *it is* he *that* hath made us, and not we ourselves; *we are* his people, and the sheep of his pasture.

✠ Enter into his gates with thanksgiving,

and into his courts with praise: be thankful unto him, *and* bless his name.

For the LORD *is* good; his mercy *is* everlasting; and his truth *endureth* to all generations.

✠ Praise ye the LORD. Sing unto the LORD a new song, *and* his praise in the congregation of saints.

Let Israel rejoice in him that made him: let the children of Zion be joyful in their King.

✠ Let them praise his name in the dance: let them sing praises unto him with the timbrel and harp.

For the LORD taketh pleasure in his people: he will beautify the meek with salvation.

Psalms c. 1–5; cxlix. 1–4.

VIII.

OF GOD'S WISDOM.

Fiftieth Selection.

The Unsearchable God.

CANST thou by searching find out God? canst thou find out the Almighty unto perfection?

✣ *It is* as high as heaven; what canst thou do? deeper than hell; what canst thou know?

The measure thereof *is* longer than the earth, and broader than the sea.

✣ If he cut off, and shut up, or gather together, then who can hinder him?

For he knoweth vain men: he seeth wickedness also; will he not then consider *it*?

✣ For vain man would be wise, though man be born *like* a wild ass's colt.

If thou prepare thine heart, and stretch out thine hands toward him;

✣ If iniquity *be* in thine hand, put it far

away, and let not wickedness dwell in thy tabernacles.

For then shalt thou lift up thy face without spot; yea, thou shalt be steadfast, and shalt not fear:

✛ Because thou shalt forget *thy* misery, *and* remember *it* as waters *that* pass away:

And *thine* age shall be clearer than the noonday; thou shalt shine forth, thou shalt be as the morning.

✛ And thou shalt be secure, because there is hope; yea, thou shalt dig *about thee*, *and* thou shalt take thy rest in safety.

Job xi. 7-18.

Fifty-first Selection.

The Searcher of Hearts.

O LORD, thou hast searched me, and know *me*.

✛ Thou knowest my downsitting and mine uprising, thou understandest my thought afar off.

Thou compassest my path and my lying down, and art acquainted *with* all my ways.

✠ For *there is* not a word in my tongue, *but* lo, O Lord, thou knowest it altogether.

Thou hast beset me behind and before, and laid thine hand upon me.

✠ *Such* knowledge *is* too wonderful for me; it is high, I cannot *attain* unto it.

Whither shall I go from thy spirit? or whither shall I flee from thy presence?

✠ If I ascend up into heaven, thou *art* there: if I make my bed in hell, behold, thou *art there*.

If I take the wings of the morning, *and* dwell in the uttermost parts of the sea;

✠ Even there shall thy hand lead me, and thy right hand shall hold me.

If I say, Surely the darkness shall cover me; even the night shall be light about me.

✠ Yea, the darkness hideth not from thee; but the night shineth as the day:

The darkness and the light *are* both alike *to thee*.

✠ Search me, O God, and know my heart: try me, and know my thoughts:

And see if *there be any* wicked way in me, and lead me in the way everlasting.

Psalm cxxxix. 1–12, 23, 24.

Fifty-second Selection.

Where shall Wisdom be Found?

BUT where shall wisdom be found? and where *is* the place of understanding?

✢ Man knoweth not the price thereof; neither is it found in the land of the living.

The depth saith, It *is* not in me: and the sea saith: *It is* not with me.

✢ It cannot be gotten for gold, neither shall silver be weighed *for* the price thereof.

It cannot be valued with the gold of Ophir, with the precious onyx, or the sapphire.

✢ The gold and the crystal cannot equal it: and the exchange of it *shall not be for* jewels of fine gold.

No mention shall be made of coral, or of pearls: for the price of wisdom *is* above rubies.

✢ The topaz of Ethiopia shall not equal it, neither shall it be valued with pure gold.

Whence then cometh wisdom? and where *is* the place of understanding?

✢ Seeing it is hid from the eyes of all living, and kept close from the fowls of the air.

Destruction and death say, We have heard the fame thereof with our ears.

✢ God understandeth the way thereof, and he knoweth the place thereof.

For he looketh to the ends of the earth, *and* seeth under the whole heaven;

✢ To make the weight for the winds; and he weigheth the waters by measure.

When he made a decree for the rain, and a way for the lightning of the thunder:

✢ Then did he see it, and declare it; he prepared it, yea, and searched it out.

And unto man he said, Behold, the fear of the Lord, that *is* wisdom; and to depart from evil *is* understanding.

Job xxviii. 12-28.

Fifty-third Selection.

Search for Her as for Hid Treasure.

MY son, if thou wilt receive my words, and hide my commandments with thee;

✢ So that thou incline thine ear unto

wisdom, *and* apply thine heart to understanding;

Yea, if thou criest after knowledge, *and* liftest up thy voice for understanding;

✣ If thou seekest her as silver, and searchest for her as *for* hid treasures;

Then shalt thou understand the fear of the Lord, and find the knowledge of God.

✣ For the Lord giveth wisdom: out of his mouth *cometh* knowledge and understanding.

He layeth up sound wisdom for the righteous: *he is* a buckler to them that walk uprightly.

✣ He keepeth the paths of judgment, and preserveth the way of his saints.

Then shalt thou understand righteousness, and judgment, and equity: *yea*, every good path.

Proverbs ii. 1–9.

Fifty-fourth Selection.

She is More Precious than Rubies.

HAPPY *is* the man *that* findeth wisdom, and the man *that* getteth understanding:

✣ For the merchandise of it *is* better than the merchandise of silver, and the gain thereof than fine gold.

She *is* more precious than rubies: and all the things thou canst desire are not to be compared unto her.

✣ Length of days *is* in her right hand; *and* in her left hand riches and honour.

Her ways *are* ways of pleasantness, and all her paths *are* peace.

✣ She *is* a tree of life to them that lay hold upon her: and happy *is every one* that retaineth her.

The LORD by wisdom hath founded the earth; by understanding hath he established the heavens.

✣ By his knowledge the depths are broken up, and the clouds drop down the dew.

My son, let not them depart from thine eyes: keep sound wisdom and discretion:

✣ So shall they be life unto thy soul, and grace to thy neck.

Then shalt thou walk in thy way safely, and thy foot shall not stumble.

✣ When thou liest down, thou shalt not

be afraid: yea, thou shalt lie down, and thy sleep shall be sweet.

Be not afraid of sudden fear, neither of the desolation of the wicked, when it cometh.

✢ For the LORD shall be thy confidence, and shall keep thy foot from being taken.

Proverbs iii. 13-26.

Fifty-fifth Selection.

Doth not Wisdom Cry?

DOTH not wisdom cry? and understanding put forth her voice?

✢ She standeth in the top of high places, by the way in the places of the paths.

She crieth at the gates, at the entry of the city, at the coming in at the doors:

✢ Unto you, O men, I call; and my voice *is* to the sons of man.

O ye simple, understand wisdom: and, ye fools, be ye of an understanding heart.

✢ Hear; for I will speak of excellent things; and the opening of my lips *shall be* right things.

For my mouth shall speak truth; and wickedness *is* an abomination to my lips.

✠ All the words of my mouth *are* in righteousness; *there is* nothing froward or perverse in them.

They *are* all plain to him that understandeth, and right to them that find knowledge.

✠ Receive my instruction, and not silver; and knowledge rather than choice gold.

For wisdom *is* better than rubies; and all the things that may be desired are not to be compared to it.

✠ I wisdom dwell with prudence, and find out knowledge of witty inventions.

The fear of the LORD *is* to hate evil: pride, and arrogancy, and the evil way, and the froward mouth, do I hate.

✠ Counsel *is* mine, and sound wisdom: I *am* understanding; I have strength.

By me kings reign, and princes decree justice.

✠ By me princes rule, and nobles, *even* all the judges of the earth.

I love them that love me; and those that seek me early shall find me.

✠ Riches and honour *are* with me; *yea,* durable riches and righteousness.

§ 56 — Of God's Wisdom.

My fruit *is* better than gold, yea, than fine gold; and my revenue than choice silver.

✣ I lead in the way of righteousness, in the midst of the paths of judgment:

That I may cause those that love me to inherit substance; and I will fill their treasures. *Proverbs* viii. 1-21.

Fifty-sixth Selection.

Good Doctrine.

HEAR, ye children, the instruction of a father, and attend to know understanding.

✣ For I give you good doctrine, forsake ye not my law.

For I was my father's son, tender and only *beloved* in the sight of my mother.

✣ He taught me also, and said unto me, Let thine heart retain my words: keep my commandments, and live.

Get wisdom, get understanding: forget *it* not; neither decline from the words of my mouth.

✣ Forsake her not, and she shall preserve thee: love her, and she shall keep thee.

Wisdom *is* the principal thing; *therefore*

get wisdom: and with all thy getting get understanding.

✠ Exalt her, and she shall promote thee: she shall bring thee to honour, when thou dost embrace her.

She shall give to thine head an ornament of grace: a crown of glory shall she deliver to thee.

✠ Hear, O my son, and receive my sayings; and the years of thy life shall be many.

I have taught thee in the way of wisdom; I have led thee in right paths.

✠ When thou goest, thy steps shall not be straitened; and when thou runnest, thou shalt not stumble.

Take fast hold of instruction; let *her* not go: keep her; for she *is* thy life.

Proverbs iv. 1–13.

Fifty-seventh Selection.

So Teach Us to Number Our Days.

LORD, thou hast been our dwelling-place in all generations.

✠ Before the mountains were brought forth, or ever thou hadst formed the earth and the world, even from everlasting to everlasting, thou *art* God.

Thou turnest man to destruction; and sayest, Return, ye children of men.

✠ For a thousand years in thy sight *are but* as yesterday when it is past, and *as* a watch in the night.

Thou carriest them away as with a flood; they are *as* a sleep: in the morning *they are* like grass *which* groweth up.

✠ In the morning it flourisheth, and groweth up; in the evening it is cut down, and withereth.

For we are consumed by thine anger, and by thy wrath are we troubled.

✠ Thou hast set our iniquities before thee, our secret *sins* in the light of thy countenance.

For all our days are passed away in thy wrath: we spend our years as a tale *that is told*.

✠ The days of our years *are* threescore years and ten;

And if by reason of strength *they be* fourscore years, yet *is* their strength labour and sorrow; for it is soon cut off, and we fly away.

✣ Who knoweth the power of thine anger? even according to thy fear, *so is* thy wrath.

So teach *us* to number our days, that we may apply *our* hearts unto wisdom.

✣ Return, O LORD, how long? and let it repent thee concerning thy servants.

O satisfy us early with thy mercy; that we may rejoice and be glad all our days.

✣ Make us glad according to the days *wherein* thou hast afflicted us, *and* the years *wherein* we have seen evil.

Let thy work appear unto thy servants, and thy glory unto their children.

✣ And let the beauty of the LORD our God be upon us:

And establish thou the work of our hands upon us; yea, the work of our hands establish thou it.

Psalm xc. 1-17.

IX.

CHRIST AND HIS KINGDOM.

Fifty-eighth Selection.

Thou art My Son.

WHY do the heathen rage? and the people imagine a vain thing?

✠ The kings of the earth set themselves, and the rulers take counsel together,

Against the LORD, and against his anointed, *saying*,

✠ Let us break their bands asunder, and cast away their cords from us.

He that sitteth in the heavens shall laugh: the LORD shall have them in derision.

✠ Then shall he speak unto them in his wrath, and vex them in his sore displeasure.

Yet have I set my king upon my holy hill of Zion.

✠ I will declare the decree: the LORD hath said unto me, Thou *art* my Son; this day have I begotten thee.

Ask of me, and I shall give *thee* the heathen *for* thine inheritance, and the uttermost parts of the earth *for* thy possession.

✠ Thou shalt break them with a rod of iron; thou shalt dash them in pieces like a potter's vessel.

Be wise now therefore, O ye kings: be instructed, ye judges of the earth.

✠ Serve the LORD with fear, and rejoice with trembling.

Kiss the Son, lest he be angry, and ye perish *from* the way, when his wrath is kindled but a little.

✠ Blessed *are* all they that put their trust in him.

Psalm ii. 1-12.

Fifty-ninth Selection.

The Heir of All Things.

GOD, who at sundry times and in divers manners spake in time past unto the fathers by the prophets,

✠ Hath in these last days spoken unto us by *his* Son, whom he hath appointed heir of all things, by whom also he made the worlds;

Who being the brightness of *his* glory, and the express image of his person, and upholding all things by the word of his power, when he had by himself purged our sins, sat down on the right hand of the Majesty on high;

✣ Being made so much better than the angels, as he hath by inheritance obtained a more excellent name than they.

For unto which of the angels said he at any time, Thou art my Son, this day have I begotten thee? And again, I will be to him a Father, and he shall be to me a Son?

✣ And again, when he bringeth in the first-begotten into the world, he saith, And let all the angels of God worship him.

And of the angels he saith, Who maketh his angels spirits, and his ministers a flame of fire.

✣ But unto the Son, *he saith*, Thy throne, O God, *is* for ever and ever: a sceptre of righteousness *is* the sceptre of thy kingdom;

Thou hast loved righteousness, and hated iniquity; therefore God, *even* thy God, hath anointed thee with the oil of gladness above thy fellows.

✠ And, Thou, Lord, in the beginning hast laid the foundation of the earth; and the heavens are the works of thine hands.

They shall perish; but thou remainest: and they all shall wax old as doth a garment;

✠ And as a vesture shalt thou fold them up, and they shall be changed: but thou art the same, and thy years shall not fail.

Hebrews i. 1-12.

Sixtieth Selection.

Fairer than the Children of Men.

MY heart is inditing a good matter: I speak of the things which I have made touching the king: my tongue *is* the pen of a ready writer.

✠ Thou art fairer than the children of men: grace is poured into thy lips: therefore God hath blessed thee for ever.

Gird thy sword upon *thy* thigh, O *most* mighty, with thy glory and thy majesty.

✠ And in thy majesty ride prosperously, because of truth and meekness *and* righteousness; and thy right hand shall teach thee terrible things.

☩ Thine arrows *are* sharp in the heart of the king's enemies; *whereby* the people fall under thee.

Thy throne, O God, *is* for ever and ever: the sceptre of thy kingdom *is* a right sceptre.

☩ Thou lovest righteousness, and hatest wickedness: therefore God, thy God, hath anointed thee with the oil of gladness above thy fellows.

All thy garments *smell* of myrrh, and aloes, *and* cassia, out of the ivory palaces, whereby they have made thee glad.

☩ King's daughters *were* among thy honourable women: upon thy right hand did stand the queen in gold of Ophir.

Hearken, O daughter, and consider, and incline thine ear; forget also thine own people, and thy father's house;

☩ So shall the king greatly desire thy beauty: for he *is* thy Lord; and worship thou him.

And the daughter of Tyre *shall be there* with a gift; *even* the rich among the people shall entreat thy favour.

☩ The king's daughter *is* all glorious within: her clothing *is* of wrought gold.

She shall be brought unto the king in raiment of needlework; the virgins her companions that follow her shall be brought unto thee.

✠ With gladness and rejoicing shall they be brought: they shall enter into the king's palace.

Instead of thy fathers shall be thy children, whom thou mayest make princes in all the earth.

✠ I will make thy name to be remembered in all generations: therefore shall the people praise thee for ever and ever.

Psalm xlv. 1-17.

Sixty-first Selection.

Men Shall be Blessed in Him.

GIVE the king thy judgments, O God, and thy righteousness unto the king's son.

✠ He shall judge thy people with righteousness, and thy poor with judgment.

The mountains shall bring peace to the people, and the little hills, by righteousness.

✠ He shall judge the poor of the people,

he shall save the children of the needy, and shall break in pieces the oppressor.

They shall fear thee as long as the sun and moon endure, throughout all generations.

✠ He shall come down like rain upon the mown grass: as showers *that* water the earth.

In his days shall the righteous flourish; and abundance of peace so long as the moon endureth.

✠ He shall have dominion also from sea to sea, and from the river unto the ends of the earth.

They that dwell in the wilderness shall bow before him; and his enemies shall lick the dust. The kings of Tarshish and of the isles shall bring presents: the kings of Sheba and Seba shall offer gifts.

✠ Yea, all kings shall fall down before him: all nations shall serve him.

For he shall deliver the needy when he crieth; the poor also, and *him* that hath no helper.

✠ He shall spare the poor and needy, and shall save the souls of the needy.

He shall redeem their soul from deceit

and violence: and precious shall their blood be in his sight.

✠ And he shall live, and to him shall be given of the gold of Sheba: prayer also shall be made for him continually; *and* daily shall he be praised.

There shall be an handful of corn in the earth upon the top of the mountains;

✠ The fruit thereof shall shake like Lebanon: and *they* of the city shall flourish like grass of the earth.

His name shall endure for ever: his name shall be continued as long as the sun:

✠ And *men* shall be blessed in him: all nations shall call him blessed.

Blessed *be* the LORD God, the God of Israel, who only doeth wondrous things.

✠ And blessed *be* his glorious name for ever; and let the whole earth be filled *with* his glory. Amen, and Amen.

Psalm lxxii. 1-19.

Sixty-second Selection.

The Magnificat.

AND Mary said, My soul doth magnify the Lord,

✠ And my spirit hath rejoiced in God my Saviour.

For he hath regarded the low estate of his handmaiden: for behold, from henceforth all generations shall call me blessed.

✠ For he that is mighty hath done to me great things; and holy *is* his name.

And his mercy *is* on them that fear him, from generation to generation.

✠ He hath shewed strength with his arm; he hath scattered the proud in the imagination of their hearts.

He hath put down the mighty from *their* seats, and exalted them of low degree.

✠ He hath filled the hungry with good things, and the rich he hath sent empty away.

He hath holpen his servant Israel, in remembrance of *his* mercy;

✠ As he spake to our fathers, to Abraham, and to his seed, for ever. *St. Luke* i. 46–55.

Sixty-third Selection.

The Benedictus.

BLESSED *be* the Lord God of Israel; for he hath visited and redeemed his people,

✠ And hath raised up an horn of salvation for us, in the house of his servant David:

As he spake by the mouth of his holy prophets, which have been since the world began:

✠ That we should be saved from our enemies, and from the hand of all that hate us;

To perform the mercy *promised* to our fathers, and to remember his holy covenant;

✠ The oath which he sware to our father Abraham,

That he would grant unto us, that we, being delivered out of the hand of our enemies, might serve him without fear,

✠ In holiness and righteousness before him, all the days of our life.

St. Luke i. 68–75.

Sixty-fourth Selection.

The True Oblations.

HEAR, O heavens, and give ear, O earth: for the LORD hath spoken; I have nourished and brought up children, and they have rebelled against me.

✠ To what purpose is the multitude of your sacrifices unto me? saith the LORD.

Bring no more vain oblations; incense is an abomination unto me; the new moons and sabbaths, the calling of assemblies, I cannot away with; it is iniquity, even the solemn meeting.

✠ Your new moons and your appointed feasts my soul hateth; they are a trouble unto me; I am weary to bear them.

And when ye spread forth your hands, I will hide mine eyes from you: yea, when ye make many prayers, I will not hear: your hands are full of blood.

✠ Wash you, make you clean; put away the evil of your doings from before mine eyes;

Cease to do evil; learn to do well;

✠ Seek judgment, relieve the oppressed, judge the fatherless, plead for the widow.

Come now, and let us reason together, saith the LORD:

✢ Though your sins be as scarlet, they shall be as white as snow:

Though they be red like crimson, they shall be as wool.

✢ If ye be willing and obedient, ye shall eat the good of the land:

But if ye refuse and rebel, ye shall be devoured with the sword: for the mouth of the LORD hath spoken it.

Isaiah i. 2, 11, 13-20.

Sixty-fifth Selection.

The Promised Light.

THE people that walked in darkness have seen a great light: they that dwell in the land of the shadow of death, upon them hath the light shined.

✢ For unto us a child is born, unto us a son is given; and the government shall be upon his shoulder:

And his name shall be called Wonderful, Counsellor, The mighty God, The everlasting Father, The Prince of Peace.

✠ Of the increase of his government and peace there shall be no end. The zeal of the LORD of hosts will perform this.

And there shall come forth a rod out of the stem of Jesse, and a Branch shall grow out of his roots:

✠ And the spirit of the LORD shall rest upon him, the spirit of wisdom and understanding, the spirit of counsel and might, the spirit of knowledge and of the fear of the LORD;

And shall make him of quick understanding in the fear of the LORD: and he shall not judge after the sight of his eyes, neither reprove after the hearing of his ears:

✠ But with righteousness shall he judge the poor, and reprove with equity for the meek of the earth.

And righteousness shall be the girdle of his loins, and faithfulness the girdle of his reins.

✠ The wolf also shall dwell with the lamb, and the leopard shall lie down with the kid;

And the calf and the young lion and

the fatling together; and a little child shall lead them.

✢ And the cow and the bear shall feed; their young ones shall lie down together; and the lion shall eat straw like the ox.

And the sucking child shall play on the hole of the asp, and the weaned child shall put his hand on the cockatrice's den.

✢ They shall not hurt nor destroy in all my holy mountain: for the earth shall be full of the knowledge of the LORD, as the waters cover the sea.

Isaiah ix. 2, 6, 7; xi. 1–9.

Sirty-sixth Selection.

Behold My Servant.

BEHOLD my servant, whom I uphold; mine elect, in whom my soul delighteth; I have put my spirit upon him: he shall bring forth judgment to the Gentiles.

✢ He shall not cry, nor lift up, nor cause his voice to be heard in the street.

A bruised reed shall he not break, and the smoking flax shall he not quench: he shall bring forth judgment unto truth.

✣ He shall not fail nor be discouraged, till he have set judgment in the earth: and the isles shall wait for his law.

Thus saith God the Lord, he that created the heavens, and stretched them out; he that spread forth the earth, and that which cometh out of it;

✣ He that giveth breath unto the people upon it, and spirit to them that walk therein:

I the Lord have called thee in righteousness, and will hold thine hand, and will keep thee, and give thee for a covenant of the people, for a light of the Gentiles;

✣ To open the blind eyes, to bring out the prisoners from the prison, and them that sit in darkness out of the prison house.

I am the Lord: that is my name: and my glory will I not give to another, neither my praise to graven images.

✣ Behold, the former things are come to pass, and new things do I declare: before they spring forth I tell you of them.

Sing unto the Lord a new song, and his praise from the end of the earth, ye that go down to the sea, and all that is therein; the isles, and the inhabitants thereof.

✝ Let the wilderness and the cities thereof lift up their voice, the villages that Kedar doth inhabit:

Let the inhabitants of the rock sing, let them shout from the top of the mountains.

✝ Let them give glory unto the LORD, and declare his praise in the islands.

And I will bring the blind by a way that they knew not; I will lead them in paths that they have not known:

✝ I will make darkness light before them, and crooked things straight. These things will I do unto them, and not forsake them.

Isaiah xlii. 1-12, 16.

Sixty-seventh Selection.

The First-born of All Creation.

FOR this cause we also, since the day we heard *it*, do not cease to pray for you, and to desire that ye might be filled with the knowledge of his will in all wisdom and spiritual understanding;

✝ That ye might walk worthy of the

Lord unto all pleasing, being fruitful in every good work, and increasing in the knowledge of God;

Strengthened with all might, according to his glorious power, unto all patience and long-suffering with joyfulness;

✢ Giving thanks unto the Father, which hath made us meet to be partakers of the inheritance of the saints in light:

Who hath delivered us from the power of darkness, and hath translated *us* into the kingdom of his dear Son:

✢ In whom we have redemption through his blood, *even* the forgiveness of sins:

Who is the image of the invisible God, the first-born of every creature: for by him were all things created, that are in heaven, and that are in earth, visible and invisible, whether *they be* thrones, or dominions, or principalities, or powers: all things were created by him, and for him:

✢ And he is before all things, and by him all things consist.

And he is the head of the body, the church: who is the beginning, the first-born from the dead; that in all *things* he might have the pre-eminence.

✢ For it pleased *the Father* that in him should all fulness dwell;

And, having made peace through the blood of his cross, by him to reconcile all things unto himself; by him, *I say*, whether *they be* things in earth, or things in heaven.

Colossians i. 9-20.

Sixty-eighth Selection.

Surely He Hath Borne Our Griefs.

WHO hath believed our report?
✢ And to whom is the arm of the LORD revealed?

For he shall grow up before him as a tender plant, and as a root out of a dry ground: he hath no form nor comeliness;

✢ And when we shall see him, *there is* no beauty that we should desire him.

He is despised and rejected of men; a man of sorrows, and acquainted with grief:

✢ And we hid as it were *our* faces from him; he was despised, and we esteemed him not.

Surely he hath borne our griefs, and carried our sorrows:

✠ Yet we did esteem him stricken, smitten of God, and afflicted.

But he *was* wounded for our transgressions, *he was* bruised for our iniquities:

✠ The chastisement of our peace *was* upon him; and with his stripes we are healed.

All we like sheep have gone astray; we have turned every one to his own way;

✠ And the LORD hath laid on him the iniquity of us all.

He was oppressed, and he was afflicted, yet he opened not his mouth: he is brought as a lamb to the slaughter, and as a sheep before her shearers is dumb, so he openeth not his mouth.

✠ He was taken from prison and from judgment: and who shall declare his generation?

For he was cut off out of the land of the living: for the transgression of my people was he stricken.

✠ And he made his grave with the wicked, and with the rich in his death; because he had done no violence, neither *was any* deceit in his mouth.

Yet it pleased the LORD to bruise him;

he hath put *him* to grief: when thou shalt make his soul an offering for sin, he shall see *his* seed, he shall prolong *his* days, and the pleasure of the Lord shall prosper in his hand.

✠ He shall see of the travail of his soul, *and* shall be satisfied: by his knowledge shall my righteous servant justify many; for he shall bear their iniquities.

Therefore will I divide him *a portion* with the great, and he shall divide the spoil with the strong; because he hath poured out his soul unto death:

✠ And he was numbered with the transgressors; and he bare the sin of many, and made intercession for the transgressors.

Isaiah liii. 1-12.

Sixty-ninth Selection.

Perfect through Sufferings.

FOR unto the angels hath he not put in subjection the world to come whereof we speak.

✠ But one in a certain place testified, saying, What is man, that thou art mindful of him? or the son of man, that thou visitest him?

Thou madest him a little lower than the angels; thou crownedst him with glory and honour, and didst set him over the works of thy hands;

✠ Thou hast put all things in subjection under his feet.

For in that he put all in subjection under him, he left nothing *that is* not put under him.

✠ But now we see not yet all things put under him:

But we see Jesus, who was made a little lower than the angels for the suffering of death, crowned with glory and honour;

✠ That he by the grace of God should taste death for every man.

For it became him, for whom *are* all things, and by whom *are* all things, in bringing many sons unto glory, to make the Captain of their salvation perfect through sufferings.

✠ For both he that sanctifieth, and they who are sanctified, *are* all of one: for which cause he is not ashamed to call them brethren,

Saying, I will declare thy name unto my brethren, in the midst of the church will I sing praise unto thee.

Hebrews ii. 5-12.

Seventieth Selection.

Prepare Ye the Way of the Lord.

COMFORT ye, comfort ye my people, saith your God. Speak ye comfortably to Jerusalem, and cry unto her, that her warfare is accomplished, that her iniquity is pardoned:

✠ For she hath received of the LORD's hand double for all her sins.

The voice of him that crieth in the wilderness, Prepare ye the way of the LORD, make straight in the desert a highway for our God.

✠ Every valley shall be exalted, and every mountain and hill shall be made low:

And the crooked shall be made straight, and the rough places plain:

✠ And the glory of the LORD shall be revealed, and all flesh shall see *it* together: for the mouth of the LORD hath spoken *it*.

The voice said, Cry. And he said, What shall I cry?

✠ All flesh *is* grass, and all the goodliness thereof *is* as the flower of the field:

The grass withereth, the flower fadeth: because the spirit of the LORD bloweth upon it: surely the people *is* grass.

✠ The grass withereth, the flower fadeth: but the word of our God shall stand for ever.

O Zion, that bringest good tidings, get thee up into the high mountain;

✠ O Jerusalem, that bringest good tidings, lift up thy voice with strength; lift *it* up, be not afraid; say unto the cities of Judah, Behold your God!

Behold, the Lord GOD will come with strong *hand*, and his arm shall rule for him:

✠ Behold, his reward *is* with him, and his work before him.

He shall feed his flock like a shepherd: he shall gather the lambs with his arm, and carry *them* in his bosom, *and* shall gently lead those that are with young.

Isaiah xl. 1-11.

Seventy-first Selection.

The Messenger of Good Tidings.

HOW beautiful upon the mountains are the feet of him that bringeth good tidings, that publisheth peace; that bringeth good tidings of good, that publisheth salvation; that saith unto Zion, Thy God reigneth!

✢ Thy watchmen shall lift up the voice; with the voice together shall they sing: for they shall see eye to eye, when the Lord shall bring again Zion.

Break forth into joy, sing together, ye waste places of Jerusalem: for the Lord hath comforted his people, he hath redeemed Jerusalem.

✢ The Lord hath made bare his holy arm in the eyes of all the nations; and all the ends of the earth shall see the salvation of our God.

Depart ye, depart ye, go ye out from thence, touch no unclean *thing;* go ye out of the midst of her; be ye clean, that bear the vessels of the Lord.

✢ For ye shall not go out with haste, nor

go by flight: for the Lord will go before you; and the God of Israel *will be* your rearward.

Behold, my servant shall deal prudently, he shall be exalted and extolled, and be very high.

✠ As many were astonied at thee; his visage was so marred more than any man, and his form more than the sons of men:

So shall he sprinkle many nations; the kings shall shut their mouths at him: for *that* which had not been told them shall they see; and *that* which they had not heard shall they consider.

Isaiah lii. 7–15.

Seventy-second Selection.

The Spirit of the Lord shall Rest upon Him.

AND there shall come forth a rod out of the stem of Jesse, and a Branch shall grow out of his roots:

✠ And the spirit of the Lord shall rest upon him, the spirit of wisdom and understanding, the spirit of counsel and might, the spirit of knowledge and of the fear of the Lord;

And shall make him of quick understanding in the fear of the Lord: and he shall not judge after the sight of his eyes, neither reprove after the hearing of his ears:

✠ But with righteousness shall he judge the poor, and reprove with equity for the meek of the earth:

And he shall smite the earth with the rod of his mouth, and with the breath of his lips shall he slay the wicked.

✠ And righteousness shall be the girdle of his loins, and faithfulness the girdle of his reins.

The wolf also shall dwell with the lamb, and the leopard shall lie down with the kid; and the calf and the young lion and the fatling together; and a little child shall lead them.

✠ And in that day thou shalt say, O Lord, I will praise thee: though thou wast angry with me, thine anger is turned away, and thou comfortedst me.

Behold, God *is* my salvation; I will trust, and not be afraid: for the Lord JEHOVAH *is* my strength and *my* song; he also is become my salvation.

✠ Therefore with joy shall ye draw water out of the wells of salvation.

And in that day shall ye say, Praise the Lord, call upon his name, declare his doings among the people, make mention that his name is exalted.

✠ Sing unto the Lord; for he hath done excellent things: this *is* known in all the earth.

Cry out and shout, thou inhabitant of Zion: for great *is* the Holy One of Israel in the midst of thee.

Isaiah xi. 1-6; xii. 1-6.

Seventy-third Selection.

The Lord hath Anointed Me.

THE Spirit of the Lord God *is* upon me; because the Lord hath anointed me to preach good tidings unto the meek; he hath sent me to bind up the brokenhearted, to proclaim liberty to the captives, and the opening of the prison to *them that are* bound;

✠ To proclaim the acceptable year of the Lord, and the day of vengeance of our God; to comfort all that mourn;

To appoint unto them that mourn in Zion, to give unto them beauty for ashes, the oil of joy for mourning, the garment of praise for the spirit of heaviness; that they might be called trees of righteousness, the planting of the LORD, that he might be glorified.

✠ And they shall build the old wastes, they shall raise up the former desolations, and they shall repair the waste cities, the desolations of many generations.

And strangers shall stand and feed your flocks, and the sons of the alien *shall be* your plowmen and your vinedressers.

✠ But ye shall be named the Priests of the LORD: *men* shall call you the Ministers of our God:

Ye shall eat the riches of the Gentiles, and in their glory shall ye boast yourselves.

✠ For your shame *ye shall have* double; and *for* confusion they shall rejoice in their portion: therefore in their land they shall possess the double: everlasting joy shall be unto them.

For I the LORD love judgment, I hate robbery for burnt offering; and I will direct their work in truth, and I will make an everlasting covenant with them.

☩ And their seed shall be known among the Gentiles, and their offspring among the people: all that see them shall acknowledge them, that they *are* the seed *which* the LORD hath blessed.

I will greatly rejoice in the LORD, my soul shall be joyful in my God; for he hath clothed me with the garments of salvation, he hath covered me with the robe of righteousness, as a bridegroom decketh *himself* with ornaments, and as a bride adorneth *herself* with her jewels.

☩ For as the earth bringeth forth her bud, and as the garden causeth the things that are sown in it to spring forth; so the Lord GOD will cause righteousness and praise to spring forth before all the nations.

Isaiah lxi. 1–11.

Seventy-fourth Selection.

The Covenant of Peace.

THUS saith the LORD, the Redeemer of Israel, *and* his Holy One, to him whom man despiseth, to him whom the nation abhorreth, to a servant of rulers,

✠ Kings shall see and arise, princes also shall worship, because of the LORD that is faithful, *and* the Holy One of Israel, and he shall choose thee.

Thus saith the LORD, In an acceptable time have I heard thee, and in a day of salvation have I helped thee:

✠ And I will preserve thee, and give thee for a covenant of the people, to establish the earth, to cause to inherit the desolate heritages;

That thou mayest say to the prisoners, Go forth; to them that *are* in darkness, Shew yourselves.

✠ They shall feed in the ways, and their pastures *shall be* in all high places.

They shall not hunger nor thirst; neither shall the heat nor sun smite them:

✠ For he that hath mercy on them shall lead them, even by the springs of water shall he guide them.

And I will make all my mountains a way, and my highways shall be exalted.

✠ Behold, these shall come from far: and, lo, these from the north and from the west; and these from the land of Sinim.

Sing, O heavens; and be joyful, O earth; and break forth into singing, O mountains:

✣ For the Lord hath comforted his people, and will have mercy upon his afflicted.

Isaiah xlix. 7-13.

Seventy-fifth Selection.

Our Peace.

WHEREFORE remember, that ye *being* in time past Gentiles in the flesh, who are called Uncircumcision by that which is called the Circumcision in the flesh made by hands;

✣ That at that time ye were without Christ, being aliens from the commonwealth of Israel, and strangers from the covenants of promise, having no hope, and without God in the world:

But now, in Christ Jesus, ye, who sometimes were far off, are made nigh by the blood of Christ.

✣ For he is our peace, who hath made

both one, and hath broken down the middle wall of partition *between us;*

Having abolished in his flesh the enmity, *even* the law of commandments *contained* in ordinances: for to make in himself of twain one new man, *so* making peace;

✠ And that he might reconcile both unto God in one body by the cross, having slain the enmity thereby:

And came and preached peace to you which were afar off, and to them that were nigh.

✠ For through him we both have access by one Spirit unto the Father.

Now therefore ye are no more strangers and foreigners, but fellow-citizens with the saints, and of the household of God;

✠ And are built upon the foundation of apostles and prophets, Jesus Christ himself being the chief corner-*stone;*

In whom all the building fitly framed together, groweth unto an holy temple in the Lord:

✠ In whom ye also are builded together, for an habitation of God through the Spirit.

Ephesians ii. 11–22.

Seventy-sixth Selection.

The Joy of the Whole Earth.

GREAT *is* the LORD, and greatly to be praised in the city of our God, *in* the mountain of his holiness.

✠ Beautiful for situation, the joy of the whole earth, *is* mount Zion, *on* the sides of the north, the city of the great king.

God is known in her palaces for a refuge.

✠ For, lo, the kings were assembled, they passed by together.

They saw *it, and* so they marvelled; they were troubled, *and* hasted away.

✠ Fear took hold upon them there, *and* pain, as of a woman in travail.

Thou breakest the ships of Tarshish with an east wind.

✠ As we have heard, so have we seen in the city of the LORD of hosts, in the city of our God: God will establish it for ever.

We have thought of thy loving-kindness, O God, in the midst of thy temple.

✠ According to thy name, O God, so *is* thy praise unto the ends of the earth: thy right hand is full of righteousness.

Let mount Zion rejoice, let the daughters of Judah be glad, because of thy judgments.

✠ Walk about Zion, and go round about her: tell the towers thereof.

Mark ye well her bulwarks, consider her palaces; that ye may tell *it* to the generation following.

✠ For this God *is* our God for ever and ever: he will be our guide *even* unto death.

Psalm xlviii. 1-14.

Seventy-seventh Selection.

Great Shall be the Peace of Thy Children.

O THOU afflicted, tossed with tempest, *and* not comforted, behold, I will lay thy stones with fair colours, and lay thy foundations with sapphires.

✠ And I will make thy windows of agates, and thy gates of carbuncles, and all thy borders of pleasant stones.

And all thy children *shall be* taught of the LORD;

✠ And great *shall be* the peace of thy children.

In righteousness shalt thou be established: thou shalt be far from oppression; for thou shalt not fear: and from terror; for it shall not come near thee.

✢ Behold, they shall surely gather together, *but* not by me: whosoever shall gather together against thee shall fall for thy sake.

Behold, I have created the smith that bloweth the coals in the fire, and that bringeth forth an instrument for his work; and I have created the waster to destroy.

✢ No weapon that is formed against thee shall prosper; and every tongue *that* shall rise against thee in judgment thou shalt condemn.

This *is* the heritage of the servants of the Lord, and their righteousness *is* of me, saith the Lord.

Isaiah liv. 11-17.

Seventy-eighth Selection.

They Shall Obtain Joy and Gladness.

THE wilderness and the solitary place shall be glad for them; and the desert shall rejoice, and blossom as the rose.

✠ It shall blossom abundantly, and rejoice even with joy and singing:

The glory of Lebanon shall be given unto it, the excellency of Carmel and Sharon;

✠ They shall see the glory of the LORD, *and* the excellency of our God.

Strengthen ye the weak hands, and confirm the feeble knees.

✠ Say to them *that are* of a fearful heart, Be strong, fear not:

Behold, your God will come *with* vengeance, *even* God *with* a recompence; he will come and save you.

✠ Then the eyes of the blind shall be opened, and the ears of the deaf shall be unstopped.

Then shall the lame *man* leap as an hart, and the tongue of the dumb sing: for in the wilderness shall waters break out, and streams in the desert.

✠ And the parched ground shall become a pool, and the thirsty land springs of water: in the habitation of dragons, where each lay, *shall be* grass with reeds and rushes.

And an highway shall be there, and a way, and it shall be called The way of holiness; the unclean shall not pass over it; but it *shall be* for those: the wayfaring men, though fools, shall not err *therein.*

✟ No lion shall be there, nor *any* ravenous beast shall go up thereon, it shall not be found there; but the redeemed shall walk *there:* —

And the ransomed of the LORD shall return, and come to Zion with songs and everlasting joy upon their heads:

✟ They shall obtain joy and gladness, and sorrow and sighing shall flee away.

Isaiah xxxv. 1–10.

Seventy-ninth Selection.

Arise, Shine, for Thy Light is Come.

ARISE, shine; for thy light is come, and the glory of the LORD is risen upon thee.

✟ For, behold, the darkness shall cover the earth, and gross darkness the people:

But the LORD shall arise upon thee, and his glory shall be seen upon thee.

✟ And the Gentiles shall come to thy light, and kings to the brightness of thy rising.

Lift up thine eyes round about, and see: all they gather themselves together, they come to thee:

✠ Thy sons shall come from far, and thy daughters shall be nursed at *thy* side.

Then thou shalt see, and flow together, and thine heart shall fear, and be enlarged;

✠ Because the abundance of the sea shall be converted unto thee, the forces of the Gentiles shall come unto thee.

For brass I will bring gold, and for iron I will bring silver, and for wood brass, and for stones iron:

✠ I will also make thy officers peace, and thine exactors righteousness.

Violence shall no more be heard in thy land, wasting nor destruction within thy borders;

✠ But thou shalt call thy walls Salvation, and thy gates Praise.

The sun shall be no more thy light by day; neither for brightness shall the moon give light unto thee:

✠ But the Lord shall be unto thee an everlasting light, and thy God thy glory.

Thy sun shall no more go down; neither shall thy moon withdraw itself:

✣ For the LORD shall be thine everlasting light, and the days of thy mourning shall be ended.

Thy people also *shall be* all righteous: they shall inherit the land for ever, the branch of my planting, the work of my hands, that I may be glorified.

✣ A little one shall become a thousand, and a small one a strong nation: I the LORD will hasten it in his time.

Isaiah lx. 1-5, 17-22.

Eightieth Selection.

The Gospel of Peace.

FOR Christ *is* the end of the law for righteousness to every one that believeth.

✣ For Moses describeth the righteousness which is of the law, That the man which doeth those things shall live by them.

But the righteousness which is of faith speaketh on this wise, Say not in thine heart, Who shall ascend into heaven? (that is, to bring Christ down *from above:*)

✢ Or, who shall descend into the deep? (that is, to bring up Christ again from the dead.)

But what saith it? The word is nigh thee, *even* in thy mouth, and in thy heart: that is, the word of faith, which we preach:

✢ That if thou shalt confess with thy mouth the Lord Jesus, and shalt believe in thine heart that God hath raised him from the dead, thou shalt be saved.

For with the heart man believeth unto righteousness; and with the mouth confession is made unto salvation.

✢ For the Scripture saith, Whosoever believeth on him shall not be ashamed.

For there is no difference between the Jew and the Greek: for the same Lord over all is rich unto all that call upon him.

✢ For whosoever shall call upon the name of the Lord shall be saved.

How then shall they call on him in whom they have not believed? and how shall they believe in him of whom they have not heard? and how shall they hear without a preacher?

✚ And how shall they preach, except they be sent? as it is written, How beautiful are the feet of them that preach the gospel of peace, and bring glad tidings of good things!
Romans x. 4-15.

Eighty-first Selection.

The Invitation.

HO, every one that thirsteth, come ye to the waters, and he that hath no money; come ye, buy, and eat;

✚ Yea, come, buy wine and milk without money and without price.

Wherefore do ye spend money for *that which is* not bread? and your labour for *that which* satisfieth not?

✚ Hearken diligently unto me, and eat ye *that which is* good, and let your soul delight itself in fatness.

Incline your ear, and come unto me: hear, and your soul shall live;

✚ And I will make an everlasting covenant with you, *even* the sure mercies of David.

Behold, I have given him *for* a witness

to the people, a leader and commander to the people.

✠ Behold, thou shalt call a nation *that* thou knowest not, and nations *that* knew not thee shall run unto thee because of the Lord thy God, and for the Holy One of Israel; for he hath glorified thee.

Seek ye the Lord while he may be found, call ye upon him while he is near: let the wicked forsake his way, and the unrighteous man his thoughts:

✠ And let him return unto the Lord, and he will have mercy upon him; and to our God, for he will abundantly pardon.

For my thoughts *are* not your thoughts, neither *are* your ways my ways, saith the Lord.

✠ For *as* the heavens are higher than the earth, so are my ways higher than your ways, and my thoughts than your thoughts.

For as the rain cometh down, and the snow from heaven, and returneth not thither, but watereth the earth, and maketh it bring forth and bud, that it may give seed to the sower, and bread to the eater:

✠ So shall my word be that goeth forth

out of my mouth: it shall not return unto me void, but it shall accomplish that which I please, and it shall prosper *in the thing* whereto I sent it.

For ye shall go out with joy, and be led forth with peace:

✠ The mountains and the hills shall break forth before you into singing, and all the trees of the field shall clap *their* hands.

Instead of the thorn shall come up the fir tree, and instead of the brier shall come up the myrtle tree:

✠ And it shall be to the Lord for a name, for an everlasting sign *that* shall not be cut off.

Isaiah lv. 1–13.

X.

THE SPIRIT OF LIFE.

Eighty-second Selection.

The Spirit Beareth Witness.

THE Spirit itself beareth witness with our spirit, that we are the children of God: and if children, then heirs; heirs of God, and joint-heirs of Christ;

✚ If so be that we suffer with *him*, that we may be also glorified together.

For I reckon that the sufferings of this present time *are* not worthy *to be compared* with the glory which shall be revealed in us.

✚ For the earnest expectation of the creature waiteth for the manifestation of the sons of God.

For the creature was made subject to vanity, not willingly, but by reason of him who hath subjected *the same* in hope,

✚ Because the creature itself also shall be delivered from the bondage of corruption into the glorious liberty of the children of God.

For we know that the whole creation groaneth and travaileth in pain together until now.

✟ And not only *they*, but ourselves also, which have the firstfruits of the Spirit, even we ourselves groan within ourselves, waiting for the adoption, *to wit*, the redemption of our body.

For we are saved by hope: but hope that is seen is not hope: for what a man seeth, why doth he yet hope for?

✟ But if we hope for that we see not, *then* do we with patience wait for *it*.

Likewise the Spirit also helpeth our infirmities: for we know not what we should pray for as we ought:

✟ But the Spirit itself maketh intercession for us with groanings which cannot be uttered.

And he that searcheth the hearts knoweth what *is* the mind of the Spirit, because he maketh intercession for the saints according to *the will of* God.

✟ And we know that all things work together for good to them that love God, to them who are the called according to *his* purpose.

Romans viii. 16–28.

Eighty-third Selection.

The Law of The Spirit.

THERE *is* therefore now no condemnation to them which are in Christ Jesus, who walk not after the flesh, but after the Spirit.

✠ For the law of the Spirit of life in Christ Jesus hath made me free from the law of sin and death.

For what the law could not do, in that it was weak through the flesh, God sending his own Son in the likeness of sinful flesh, and for sin, condemned sin in the flesh:

✠ That the righteousness of the law might be fulfilled in us, who walk not after the flesh, but after the Spirit.

For they that are after the flesh do mind the things of the flesh; but they that are after the Spirit the things of the Spirit.

✠ For to be carnally minded *is* death; but to be spiritually minded *is* life and peace.

Because the carnal mind *is* enmity against God: for it is not subject to the law of God, neither indeed can be.

✣ So then they that are in the flesh cannot please God.

But ye are not in the flesh, but in the Spirit, if so be that the Spirit of God dwell in you.

✣ Now if any man have not the Spirit of Christ, he is none of his.

And if Christ *be* in you, the body *is* dead because of sin;

✣ But the Spirit *is* life because of righteousness.

But if the Spirit of him that raised up Jesus from the dead dwell in you, he that raised up Christ from the dead shall also quicken your mortal bodies by his Spirit that dwelleth in you.
Romans viii. 1-11.

Eighty-fourth Selection.

The Ministration of the Spirit.

BUT if the ministration of death, written *and* engraven in stones, was glorious, so that the children of Israel could not steadfastly behold the face of Moses for the glory of his countenance; which *glory* was to be done away:

✣ How shall not the ministration of the spirit be rather glorious?

For if the ministration of condemnation *be* glory, much more doth the ministration of righteousness exceed in glory.

✣ For even that which was made glorious had no glory in this respect, by reason of the glory that excelleth.

For if that which is done away *was* glorious, much more that which remaineth *is* glorious.

✣ Seeing then that we have such hope, we use great plainness of speech:

And not as Moses, *which* put a vail over his face, that the children of Israel could not steadfastly look to the end of that which is abolished:

✣ But their minds were blinded:

For until this day remaineth the same vail untaken away in the reading of the old testament; which *vail* is done away in Christ.

✣ But even unto this day, when Moses is read, the vail is upon their heart.

Nevertheless, when it shall turn to the Lord, the vail shall be taken away.

✣ Now the Lord is that Spirit: and

where the Spirit of the Lord *is*, there *is* liberty.

But we all, with open face beholding as in a glass the glory of the Lord, are changed into the same image from glory to glory, *even* as by the Spirit of the Lord.

2 *Corinthians* iii. 7–18.

Eighty-fifth Selection.

The Fruits of the Spirit.

FOR, brethren, ye have been called unto liberty; only *use* not liberty for an occasion to the flesh, but by love serve one another.

✢ For all the law is fulfilled in one word, *even* in this; Thou shalt love thy neighbour as thyself.

But if ye bite and devour one another, take heed that ye be not consumed one of another.

✢ *This* I say then, Walk in the Spirit, and ye shall not fulfil the lust of the flesh.

For the flesh lusteth against the Spirit, and the Spirit against the flesh: and these are contrary the one to the other; so that ye cannot do the things that ye would.

✠ But if ye be led of the Spirit, ye are not under the law.

Now the works of the flesh are manifest, which are *these*, Adultery, fornication, uncleanness, lasciviousness,

✠ Idolatry, witchcraft, hatred, variance, emulations, wrath, strife, seditions, heresies,

Envyings, murders, drunkenness, revellings, and such like: of the which I tell you before, as I have also told *you* in time past, that they which do such things shall not inherit the kingdom of God.

✠ But the fruit of the Spirit is love, joy, peace, longsuffering, gentleness, goodness, faith, meekness, temperance:

Against such there is no law. And they that are Christ's have crucified the flesh with the affections and lusts.

✠ If we live in the Spirit, let us also walk in the Spirit.

Galatians v. 13-25.

Eighty-sixth Selection.

The Unity of the Spirit.

NOW there are diversities of gifts, but the same Spirit.

✢ And there are differences of administrations, but the same Lord.

And there are diversities of operations, but it is the same God which worketh all in all.

✢ But the manifestation of the Spirit is given to every man to profit withal.

For to one is given by the Spirit the word of wisdom; to another the word of knowledge by the same Spirit;

✢ To another faith by the same Spirit; to another the gifts of healing by the same Spirit;

To another the working of miracles; to another prophecy; to another discerning of spirits; to another *divers* kinds of tongues; to another the interpretation of tongues:

✢ But all these worketh that one and the selfsame Spirit, dividing to every man severally as he will.

For as the body is one, and hath many members, and all the members of that one body, being many, are one body : so also *is* Christ.

✠ For by one Spirit are we all baptized into one body, whether *we be* Jews or Gentiles, whether *we be* bond or free ; and have been all made to drink into one Spirit.

There is one body, and one Spirit, even as ye are called in one hope of your calling ;

✠ One Lord, one faith, one baptism,

One God and Father of all, who *is* above all, and through all, and in you all.

1 *Corinthians* xii. 4-13 ; *Ephesians* iv. 4-6.

XI.

TRUE RELIGION.

Eighty-seventh Selection.

The Fast that God hath Chosen.

CRY aloud, spare not, lift up thy voice like a trumpet, and shew my people their transgression, and the house of Jacob their sins.

✣ Yet they seek me daily, and delight to know my ways, as a nation that did righteousness, and forsook not the ordinance of their God:

They ask of me the ordinances of justice; they take delight in approaching to **God**.

✣ Wherefore have we fasted, *say they*, and thou seest not? *wherefore* have we afflicted our soul, and thou takest no knowledge?

Behold, in the day of your fast ye find pleasure, and exact all your labours.

✣ Behold, ye fast for strife and debate, and to smite with the fist of wickedness:

ye shall not fast as *ye do this* day, to make your voice to be heard on high.

Is it such a fast that I have chosen? a day for a man to afflict his soul? *is it* to bow down his head as a bulrush, and to spread sackcloth and ashes *under him?* wilt thou call this a fast, and an acceptable day to the Lord?

✠ *Is* not this the fast that I have chosen? to loose the bands of wickedness, to undo the heavy burdens, and to let the oppressed go free, and that ye break every yoke?

Is it not to deal thy bread to the hungry, and that thou bring the poor that are cast out to thy house? when thou seest the naked, that thou cover him; and that thou hide not thyself from thine own flesh?

✠ Then shall thy light break forth as the morning, and thine health shall spring forth speedily:

And thy righteousness shall go before thee; the glory of the Lord shall be thy rearward.

✠ Then shalt thou call, and the Lord shall answer; thou shalt cry, and he shall say, Here I *am*.

Isaiah lviii. 1–9.

Eighty-eighth Selection.

God shall Judge His People.

THE mighty God, *even* the LORD, hath spoken, and called the earth from the rising of the sun unto the going down thereof.

✠ Out of Zion, the perfection of beauty, God hath shined.

Our God shall come, and shall not keep silence: a fire shall devour before him, and it shall be very tempestuous round about him.

✠ He shall call to the heavens from above, and to the earth, that he may judge his people.

Gather my saints together unto me; those that have made a covenant with me by sacrifice.

✠ And the heavens shall declare his righteousness: for God *is* judge himself.

Hear, O my people, and I will speak; O Israel, and I will testify against thee: I *am* God, *even* thy God.

✠ I will not reprove thee for thy sacrifices or thy burnt-offerings, *to have been* continually before me.

I will take no bullock out of thy house, *nor* he-goats out of thy folds.

✠ For every beast of the forest *is* mine, *and* the cattle upon a thousand hills.

I know all the fowls of the mountains: and the wild beasts of the field *are* mine.

✠ If I were hungry, I would not tell thee: for the world *is* mine, and the fulness thereof.

Will I eat the flesh of bulls, or drink the blood of goats?

✠ Offer unto God thanksgiving; and pay thy vows unto the Most High:

And call upon me in the day of trouble: I will deliver thee, and thou shalt glorify me.

Psalm l. 1-15.

Eighty-ninth Selection.

Pure Religion and Undefiled.

Do not err, my beloved brethren. Every good gift and every perfect gift is from above, and cometh down from the Father of lights, with whom is no variableness, neither shadow of turning.

✠ Of his own will begat he us with the word of truth, that we should be a kind of firstfruits of his creatures.

Wherefore, my beloved brethren, let every man be swift to hear, slow to speak, slow to wrath:

✠ For the wrath of man worketh not the righteousness of God.

Wherefore, lay apart all filthiness and superfluity of naughtiness, and receive with meekness the engrafted word, which is able to save your souls.

✠ But be ye doers of the word, and not hearers only, deceiving your own selves.

For if any be a hearer of the word, and not a doer, he is like unto a man beholding his natural face in a glass:

✠ For he beholdeth himself, and goeth his way, and straightway forgetteth what manner of man he was.

But whoso looketh into the perfect law of liberty, and continueth *therein*,

✠ He being not a forgetful hearer, but a doer of the work, this man shall be blessed in his deed.

If any man among you seem to be religious, and bridleth not his tongue, but deceiveth his own heart, this man's religion *is* vain.

✛ Pure religion and undefiled before God and the Father is this, To visit the fatherless and widows in their affliction, *and* to keep himself unspotted from the world.

James i. 16-27.

Ninetieth Selection.

Add to Your Faith Virtue.

GRACE and peace be multiplied unto you through the knowledge of God, and of Jesus our Lord,

✛ According as his divine power hath given unto us all things that *pertain* unto life and godliness, through the knowledge of him that hath called us to glory and virtue:

Whereby are given unto us exceeding great and precious promises; that by these ye might be partakers of the divine nature, having escaped the corruption that is in the world through lust.

✛ And beside this, giving all diligence,

add to your faith virtue; and to virtue knowledge;

And to knowledge temperance; and to temperance patience; and to patience godliness;

✚ And to godliness brotherly kindness; and to brotherly kindness charity.

For if these things be in you, and abound, they make *you that ye shall* neither *be* barren nor unfruitful in the knowledge of our Lord Jesus Christ.

✚ But he that lacketh these things is blind, and cannot see afar off, and hath forgotten that he was purged from his old sins.

Wherefore the rather, brethren, give diligence to make your calling and election sure: for if he do these things, ye shall never fall:

✚ For so an entrance shall be ministered unto you abundantly into the everlasting kingdom of our Lord and Saviour Jesus Christ.

2 Peter i. 2-11.

XII.

THE LAW OF GOD.

Ninety-first Selection.

Blessed are the Undefiled.

BLESSED *are* the undefiled in the way, who walk in the law of the Lord.

✣ Blessed *are* they that keep his testimonies, *and that* seek him with the whole heart.

They also do no iniquity; they walk in his ways.

✣ Thou hast commanded *us* to keep thy precepts diligently.

O that my ways were directed to keep thy statutes!

✣ Then shall I not be ashamed, when I have respect unto all thy commandments.

I will praise thee with uprightness of heart, when I shall have learned thy righteous judgments.

✣ I will keep thy statutes: O forsake me not utterly.

Wherewithal shall a young man cleanse his way? By taking heed *thereto* according to thy word.

✠ With my whole heart have I sought thee: O let me not wander from thy commandments.

Thy word have I hid in my heart, that I might not sin against thee.

✠ Blessed *art* thou, O LORD: teach me thy statutes.

With my lips have I declared all the judgments of thy mouth.

✠ I have rejoiced in the way of thy testimonies, as *much as* in all riches.

I will meditate in thy precepts, and have respect unto thy ways.

✠ I will delight myself in thy statutes: I will not forget thy word.

Psalm cxix. 1-16.

Ninety-second Selection.

Thy Testimonies are My Delight.

DEAL bountifully with thy servant, *that* I may live, and keep thy word.

✠ Open thou mine eyes, that I may behold wondrous things out of thy law.

I *am* a stranger in the earth: hide not thy commandments from me.

✛ My soul breaketh for the longing *that it hath* unto thy judgments at all times.

Thou hast rebuked the proud *that are* cursed, which do err from thy commandments.

✛ Remove from me reproach and contempt; for I have kept thy testimonies.

Princes also did sit *and* speak against me: *but* thy servant did meditate in thy statutes.

✛ Thy testimonies also *are* my delight *and* my counsellors.

Psalm cxix. 17–24.

Ninety-third Selection.

The Way of Truth.

MY soul cleaveth unto the dust: quicken thou me according to thy word.

✛ I have declared my ways, and thou heardest me: teach me thy statutes.

Make me to understand the way of thy precepts: so shall I talk of thy wondrous works.

✝ My soul melteth for heaviness: strengthen thou me according unto thy word.

Remove from me the way of lying: and grant me thy law graciously.

✝ I have chosen the way of truth: thy judgments have I laid *before me*.

I have stuck unto thy testimonies: O Lord, put me not to shame.

✝ I will run the way of thy commandments, when thou shalt enlarge my heart.
Psalm cxix. 25–32.

Ninety-fourth Selection.

This is My Comfort.

REMEMBER the word unto thy servant, upon which thou hast caused me to hope.

✝ This *is* my comfort in my affliction: for thy word hath quickened me.

The proud have had me greatly in derision: *yet* have I not declined from thy law.

✝ I remembered thy judgments of old, O Lord; and have comforted myself.

Horror hath taken hold upon me because of the wicked that forsake thy law.

✣ Thy statutes have been my songs in the house of my pilgrimage.

I have remembered thy name, O LORD, in the night, and have kept thy law.

✣ This I had, because I kept thy precepts.

Thou art my portion, O LORD: I have said that I would keep thy words.

✣ I entreated thy favour with *my* whole heart: be merciful unto me according to thy word.

I thought on my ways, and turned my feet unto thy testimonies.

✣ I made haste, and delayed not to keep thy commandments.

The bands of the wicked have robbed me: *but* I have not forgotten thy law.

✣ At midnight I will rise to give thanks unto thee, because of thy righteous judgments.

I *am* a companion of all *them* that fear thee, and of them that keep thy precepts.

✣ The earth, O LORD, is full of thy mercy: teach me thy statutes.

Psalm cxix. 49–64.

Ninety-fifth Selection.

Teach me Good Judgment.

THOU hast dealt well with thy servant, O LORD, according unto thy word.

✠ Teach me good judgment and knowledge: for I have believed thy commandments.

Before I was afflicted I went astray: but now have I kept thy word.

✠ Thou *art* good, and doest good; teach me thy statutes.

The proud have forged a lie against me: *but* I will keep thy precepts with *my* whole heart.

✠ Their heart is as fat as grease; *but* I delight in thy law.

It is good for me that I have been afflicted; that I might learn thy statutes.

✠ The law of thy mouth *is* better unto me than thousands of gold and silver.

Thy hands have made me and fashioned me: give me understanding, that I may learn thy commandments.

✠ They that fear thee will be glad when they see me; because I have hoped in thy word.

I know, O LORD, that thy judgments *are* right, and *that* thou in faithfulness hast afflicted me.

✢ Let, I pray thee, thy merciful kindness be for my comfort, according to thy word unto thy servant.

Let thy tender mercies come unto me, that I may live: for thy law *is* my delight.

✢ Let the proud be ashamed; for they dealt perversely with me without a cause: *but* I will meditate in thy precepts.

Let those that fear thee turn unto me, and those that have known thy testimonies.

✢ Let my heart be sound in thy statutes; that I be not ashamed.

Psalm cxix. 65-80.

Ninety-sixth Selection.

Thy Word is Settled in Heaven.

FOR ever, O LORD, thy word is settled in heaven.

✢ Thy faithfulness *is* unto all generations: thou hast established the earth, and it abideth.

They continue this day according to

thine ordinances: for all *are* thy servants.

✚ Unless thy law *had been* my delights, I should then have perished in mine affliction.

I will never forget thy precepts: for with them thou hast quickened me.

✚ I *am* thine, save me; for I have sought thy precepts.

The wicked have waited for me to destroy me: *but* I will consider thy testimonies.

✚ I have seen an end of all perfection: *but* thy commandment *is* exceeding broad.

Psalm cxix. 89–96.

Ninety-seventh Selection.

A Light unto My Path.

OH how love I thy law! it *is* my meditation all the day.

✚ Thou through thy commandments hast made me wiser than mine enemies: for they *are* ever with me.

I have more understanding than all my teachers: for thy testimonies *are* my meditation.

✠ I understand more than the ancients, because I keep thy precepts.

I have refrained my feet from every evil way, that I might keep thy word.

✠ I have not departed from thy judgments: for thou hast taught me.

How sweet are thy words unto my taste! *yea, sweeter* than honey to my mouth.

✠ Through thy precepts I get understanding: therefore I hate every false way.

Thy word *is* a lamp unto my feet, and a light unto my path.

✠ I have sworn, and I will perform *it*, that I will keep thy righteous judgments.

Psalm cxix. 97–106.

Ninety-eighth Selection.

Order my Steps in Thy Word.

DEAL with thy servant according unto thy mercy, and teach me thy statutes.

✠ I *am* thy servant; give me understanding, that I may know thy testimonies.

It is time for *thee*, LORD, to work: *for* they have made void thy law.

✠ Therefore I love thy commandments above gold; yea, above fine gold.

Therefore I esteem all *thy* precepts *concerning* all *things to be* right; *and* I hate every false way.

✛ Thy testimonies *are* wonderful: therefore doth my soul keep them.

The entrance of thy words giveth light; it giveth understanding unto the simple.

✛ I opened my mouth, and panted: for I longed for thy commandments.

Look thou upon me, and be merciful unto me, as thou usest to do unto those that love thy name.

✛ Order my steps in thy word: and let not any iniquity have dominion over me.

Psalm cxix. 124-133.

Ninety-ninth Selection.

Thy Word is Very Pure.

RIGHTEOUS *art* thou, O Lord, and upright *are* thy judgments.

✛ Thy testimonies *that* thou hast commanded *are* righteous and very faithful.

My zeal hath consumed me, because mine enemies have forgotten thy words.

✛ Thy word *is* very pure: therefore thy servant loveth it.

I *am* small and despised : *yet* do not I forget thy precepts.

✠ Thy righteousness *is* an everlasting righteousness, and thy law *is* the truth.

Trouble and anguish have taken hold on me : *yet* thy commandments *are* my delights.

✠ The righteousness of thy testimonies *is* everlasting : give me understanding, and I shall live.

Psalm cxix. 137–144.

One Hundredth Selection.

Consider how I Love Thy Precepts.

I CRIED with *my* whole heart ; hear me, O Lord : I will keep thy statutes.

✠ I cried unto thee : save me, and I shall keep thy testimonies.

I prevented the dawning of the morning, and cried : I hoped in thy word.

✠ Mine eyes prevent the *night*-watches, that I might meditate in thy word.

Hear my voice, according unto thy loving-kindness : O Lord, quicken me according to thy judgment.

✠ They draw nigh that follow after mischief: they are far from thy law.

Thou *art* near, O LORD; and all thy commandments *are* truth.

✠ Concerning thy testimonies I have known of old that thou hast founded them for ever.

Consider mine affliction, and deliver me: for I do not forget thy law.

✠ Plead my cause, and deliver me: quicken me according to thy word.

Salvation *is* far from the wicked: for they seek not thy statutes.

✠ Great *are* thy tender mercies, O LORD: quicken me according to thy judgments.

Many *are* my persecutors and mine enemies: *yet* do I not decline from thy testimonies.

✠ I beheld the transgressors, and was grieved; because they kept not thy word.

Consider how I love thy precepts: quicken me, O LORD, according to thy lovingkindness.

✠ Thy word *is* true *from* the beginning: and every one of thy righteous judgments *endureth* for ever.

Psalm cxix. 145–160.

One Hundred and First Selection.

My Heart Standeth in Awe.

PRINCES have persecuted me without a cause: but my heart standeth in awe of thy word.

✢ I rejoice at thy word, as one that findeth great spoil.

I hate and abhor lying: *but* thy law do I love.

✢ Seven times a day do I praise thee because of thy righteous judgments.

Great peace have they which love thy law: and nothing shall offend them.

✢ LORD, I have hoped for thy salvation, and done thy commandments.

My soul hath kept thy testimonies; and I love them exceedingly.

✢ I have kept thy precepts and thy testimonies: for all my ways *are* before thee.

Psalm cxix. 161–168.

One Hundred and Second Selection.

Let Thine Hand Help Me.

LET my cry come near before thee, O Lord: give me understanding according to thy word.

✠ Let my supplication come before thee: deliver me according to thy word.

My lips shall utter praise, when thou hast taught me thy statutes.

✠ My tongue shall speak of thy word: for all thy commandments *are* righteousness.

Let thine hand help me; for I have chosen thy precepts.

✠ I have longed for thy salvation, O Lord; and thy law *is* my delight.

Let my soul live, and it shall praise thee; and let thy judgments help me.

✠ I have gone astray like a lost sheep; seek thy servant; for I do not forget thy commandments.

Psalm cxix. 169–176.

One Hundred and Third Selection.

Return unto the Lord.

O ISRAEL, return unto the Lord thy God; for thou hast fallen by thine iniquity.

✠ Take with you words, and turn to the Lord:

Say unto him, Take away all iniquity, and receive *us* graciously: so will we render the calves of our lips.

✠ Asshur shall not save us; we will not ride upon horses:

Neither will we say any more to the work of our hands, *Ye are* our gods: for in thee the fatherless findeth mercy.

✠ I will heal their backsliding, I will love them freely: for mine anger is turned away from him.

I will be as the dew unto Israel: he shall grow as the lily, and cast forth his roots as Lebanon.

✠ His branches shall spread, and his beauty shall be as the olive-tree, and his smell as Lebanon.

They that dwell under his shadow shall return; they shall revive *as* the corn, and grow as the vine:

✠ The scent thereof *shall be* as the wine of Lebanon.

Ephraim *shall say*, What have I to do any more with idols?

✠ I have heard *him*, and observed him: I *am* like a green fir-tree. From me is thy fruit found.

Who *is* wise, and he shall understand these *things?* prudent, and he shall know them?

✠ For the ways of the LORD *are* right, and the just shall walk in them: but the transgressor shall fall therein.

Hosea xiv. 1–9.

XIII.

PENITENCE AND PARDON.

One Hundred and Fourth Selection.

Cleanse Me from My Sin.

HAVE mercy upon me, O God, according to thy loving-kindness: according unto the multitude of thy tender mercies blot out my transgressions.

✣ Wash me thoroughly from mine iniquity, and cleanse me from my sin.

For I acknowledge my transgressions: and my sin *is* ever before me. Against thee, thee only, have I sinned, and done *this* evil in thy sight:

✣ That thou mightest be justified when thou speakest, *and* be clear when thou judgest.

Hide thy face from my sins, and blot out all mine iniquities.

✣ Create in me a clean heart, O God; and renew a right spirit within me.

Cast me not away from thy presence; and take not thy Holy Spirit from me.

✠ Restore unto me the joy of thy salvation; and uphold me *with thy* free Spirit.

Then will I teach transgressors thy ways; and sinners shall be converted unto thee.

✠ Deliver me from blood-guiltiness, O God, thou God of my salvation: *and* my tongue shall sing aloud of thy righteousness.

O Lord, open thou my lips, and my mouth shall shew forth thy praise.

✠ For thou desirest not sacrifice; else would I give *it:* thou delightest not in burnt-offering.

The sacrifices of God *are* a broken spirit: a broken and a contrite heart, O God, thou wilt not despise.

Psalm li. 1-4; 9-17.

One Hundred and Fifth Selection.

There is Forgiveness with Thee.

OUT of the depths have I cried unto thee, O Lord.

✠ Lord, hear my voice: let thine ears

be attentive to the voice of my supplications.

If thou, LORD, shouldest mark iniquities, O LORD, who shall stand?

✠ But *there is* forgiveness with thee, that thou mayest be feared.

I wait for the LORD, my soul doth wait, and in his word do I hope.

✠ My soul *waiteth* for the LORD more than they that watch for the morning: *I say more than* they that watch for the morning.

Let Israel hope in the LORD: for with the LORD *there is* mercy, and with him *is* plenteous redemption.

✠ And he shall redeem Israel from all his iniquities.

Psalm cxxx. 1–8.

One Hundred and Sixth Selection.

A Prayer for the Penitent.

OH that thou wouldest rend the heavens, that thou wouldest come down,

✠ That the mountains might flow down at thy presence,

As *when* the melting fire burneth, the

fire causeth the waters to boil, to make thy name known to thine adversaries,

✛ *That* the nations may tremble at thy presence!

When thou didst terrible things *which* we looked not for, thou camest down,

✛ The mountains flowed down at thy presence.

For since the beginning of the world *men* have not heard, nor perceived by the ear,

✛ Neither hath the eye seen, O God, besides thee, *what* he hath prepared for him that waiteth for him.

Thou meetest him that rejoiceth and worketh righteousness, *those that* remember thee in thy ways:

✛ Behold, thou art wroth; for we have sinned: in those is continuance, and we shall be saved.

But we are all as an unclean *thing*, and all our righteousnesses *are* as filthy rags;

✛ And we all do fade as a leaf; and our iniquities, like the wind, have taken us away.

And *there is* none that calleth upon thy

name, that stirreth up himself to take hold of thee:

✠ For thou hast hid thy face from us, and hast consumed us, because of our iniquities.

But now, O LORD, thou *art* our Father; we *are* the clay, and thou our potter; and we all *are* the work of thy hand.

✠ Be not wroth very sore, O LORD, neither remember iniquity for ever: behold, see, we beseech thee, we *are* all thy people.

Isaiah lxiv. 1–10.

One Hundred and Seventh Selection.

If We Confess our Sins.

THIS then is the message which we have heard of him, and declare unto you, that God is light, and in him is no darkness at all.

✠ If we say that we have fellowship with him, and walk in darkness, we lie, and do not the truth:

But if we walk in the light, as he is in the light, we have fellowship one with another, and the blood of Jesus Christ his Son cleanseth us from all sin.

✢ If we say that we have no sin, we deceive ourselves, and the truth is not in us.

If we confess our sins, he is faithful and just to forgive us *our* sins, and to cleanse us from all unrighteousness.

1 *John* i. 5-9.

One Hundred and Eighth Selection.

Pardon mine Iniquity, for it is Great.

UNTO thee, O LORD, do I lift up my soul.

✢ O my God, I trust in thee: let me not be ashamed, let not mine enemies triumph over me.

Yea, let none that wait on thee be ashamed: let them be ashamed which transgress without cause.

✢ Shew me thy ways, O LORD; teach me thy paths.

Lead me in thy truth, and teach me: for thou *art* the God of my salvation; on thee do I wait all the day.

✢ Remember, O Lord, thy tender mercies and thy loving-kindnesses; for they *have been* ever of old.

Remember not the sins of my youth, nor my transgressions: according to thy mercy remember thou me for thy goodness' sake, O Lord.

✢ Good and upright *is* the Lord: therefore will he teach sinners in the way.

The meek will he guide in judgment: and the meek will he teach his way.

✢ All the paths of the Lord *are* mercy and truth unto such as keep his covenant and his testimonies.

For thy name's sake, O Lord, pardon mine iniquity; for it *is* great.

✢ What man *is* he that feareth the Lord? him shall he teach in the way *that* he shall choose.

His soul shall dwell at ease; and his seed shall inherit the earth.

✢ The secret of the Lord *is* with them that fear him; and he will shew them his covenant.

Psalm xxv. 1-14.

One Hundred and Ninth Selection.

Deliver me from my Transgressions.

I SAID, I will take heed to my ways, that I sin not with my tongue: I will keep my mouth with a bridle, while the wicked is before me.

✠ I was dumb with silence, I held my peace, *even* from good; and my sorrow was stirred.

My heart was hot within me, while I was musing the fire burned: *then* spake I with my tongue.

✠ LORD, make me to know mine end, and the measure of my days, what it *is;* *that* I may know how frail I *am.*

Behold, thou hast made my days *as* an hand-breadth; and mine age *is* as nothing before thee: verily every man at his best state *is* altogether vanity.

✠ Surely every man walketh in a vain shew: surely they are disquieted in vain: he heapeth up *riches*, and knoweth not who shall gather them.

And now, LORD, what wait I for? my hope *is* in thee.

✠ Deliver me from all my transgressions: make me not the reproach of the foolish.

I was dumb, I opened not my mouth; because thou didst *it*.

✠ Remove thy stroke away from me: I am consumed by the blow of thine hand.

When thou with rebukes dost correct man for iniquity, thou makest his beauty to consume away like a moth:

✠ Surely every man *is* vanity.

Hear my prayer, O LORD, and give ear unto my cry; hold not thy peace at my tears: for I *am* a stranger with thee, *and* a sojourner, as all my fathers *were*.

✠ O spare me, that I may recover strength, before I go hence, and be no more.

Psalm xxxix. 1-13.

One Hundred and Tenth Selection.

Enter not into Judgment.

HEAR my prayer, O LORD, give ear to my supplications: in thy faithfulness answer me, *and* in thy righteousness.

✠ And enter not into judgment with thy servant: for in thy sight shall no man living be justified.

For the enemy hath persecuted my soul; he hath smitten my life down to the ground; he hath made me to dwell in darkness, as those that have been long dead.

✠ Therefore is my spirit overwhelmed within me; my heart within me is desolate.

I remember the days of old; I meditate on all thy works; I muse on the work of thy hands.

✠ I stretch forth my hands unto thee: my soul *thirsteth* after thee, as a thirsty land.

Hear me speedily, O LORD: my spirit faileth: hide not thy face from me, lest I be like unto them that go down into the pit.

✠ Cause me to hear thy loving-kindness in the morning; for in thee do I trust: cause me to know the way wherein I should walk; for I lift up my soul unto thee.

Deliver me, O LORD, from mine enemies: I flee unto thee to hide me.

✠ Teach me to do thy will; for thou *art* my God: thy Spirit *is* good; lead me into the land of uprightness.

Quicken me, O LORD, for thy name's sake: for thy righteousness' sake bring my soul out of trouble.

Psalm cxliii. 1-11.

One Hundred and Eleventh Selection.

I Hope in Thy Word.

I AM afflicted very much: quicken me, O LORD, according unto thy word.

✠ Accept, I beseech thee, the free-will offerings of my mouth, O LORD, and teach me thy judgments.

My soul *is* continually in my hand: yet do I not forget thy law.

✠ The wicked have laid a snare for me: yet I erred not from thy precepts.

Thy testimonies have I taken as a heritage for ever: for they *are* the rejoicing of my heart.

✠ I have inclined mine heart to perform thy statutes always, *even unto* the end.

I hate *vain* thoughts: but thy law do I love.

✠ Thou *art* my hiding place and my shield: I hope in thy word.

Depart from me, ye evil doers: for I will keep the commandments of my God.

✛ Uphold me according unto thy word, that I may live: and let me not be ashamed of my hope.

Hold thou me up, and I shall be safe: and I will have respect unto thy statutes continually.

Psalm cxix. 107–117.

One Hundred and Twelfth Selection.

Thou hast Covered all their Sin.

LORD, thou hast been favorable unto thy land: thou hast brought back the captivity of Jacob.

✛ Thou hast forgiven the iniquity of thy people, thou hast covered all their sin.

Thou hast taken away all thy wrath: thou hast turned *thyself* from the fierceness of thine anger.

✛ Turn us, O God of our salvation, and cause thine anger toward us to cease.

Wilt thou be angry with us for ever? wilt thou draw out thine anger to all generations?

✚ Wilt thou not revive us again: that thy people may rejoice in thee?

Shew us thy mercy, O LORD, and grant us thy salvation.

✚ I will hear what God the LORD will speak: for he will speak peace unto his people, and to his saints: but let them not turn again to folly.

Surely his salvation *is* nigh them that fear him; that glory may dwell in our land.

✚ Mercy and truth are met together; righteousness and peace have kissed *each other*.

Truth shall spring out of the earth; and righteousness shall look down from heaven.

✚ Yea the LORD shall give *that which is* good; and our land shall yield her increase.

Righteousness shall go before him; and shall set *us* in the way of his steps.

Psalm lxxxv. 1-13.

One Hundred and Thirteenth Selection.

The Blessedness of Pardon.

BLESSED *is he whose* transgression *is* forgiven, *whose* sin *is* covered.

✚ Blessed *is* the man unto whom the

Lord imputeth not iniquity, and in whose spirit *there is* no guile.

When I kept silence, my bones waxed old through my roaring all the day long.

✠ For day and night thy hand was heavy upon me: my moisture is turned into the drought of summer.

I acknowledged my sin unto thee, and mine iniquity have I not hid. I said, I will confess my transgressions unto the Lord; and thou forgavest the iniquity of my sin.

✠ For this shall every one that is godly pray unto thee in a time when thou mayest be found: surely in the floods of great waters they shall not come nigh unto him.

Thou *art* my hiding place; thou shalt preserve me from trouble; thou shalt compass me about with songs of deliverance.

✠ I will instruct thee and teach thee in the way which thou shalt go: I will guide thee with mine eye.

Be ye not as the horse, *or* as the mule, *which* have no understanding: whose mouth must be held in with bit and bridle, lest they come near unto thee.

✠ Many sorrows *shall be* to the wicked:

but he that trusteth in the Lord, mercy shall compass him about.

Be glad in the Lord, and rejoice, ye righteous:

✢ And shout for joy, all *ye that are* upright in heart.

Psalm xxxii. 1–11.

One Hundred and Fourteenth Selection.

The Righteousness of God which is by Faith.

NOW we know that what things soever the law saith, it saith to them who are under the law:

✢ That every mouth may be stopped, and all the world may become guilty before God.

Therefore by the deeds of the law, there shall no flesh be justified in his sight: for by the law *is* the knowledge of sin.

✢ But now the righteousness of God without the law is manifested, being witnessed by the law and the prophets;

Even the righteousness of God, *which is* by faith of Jesus Christ unto all, and upon all them that believe; for there is no difference:

✠ For all have sinned, and come short of the glory of God;

Being justified freely by his grace, through the redemption that is in Christ Jesus:

✠ Whom God hath set forth *to be* a propitiation, through faith in his blood, to declare his righteousness for the remission of sins that are past, through the forbearance of God;

To declare, *I say*, at this time his righteousness: that he might be just, and the justifier of him which believeth in Jesus.

Romans iii. 19-26.

XIV.

THE JOY OF RELIGION.

One Hundred and Fifteenth Selection.

The Lord is my Shepherd.

THE LORD *is* my shepherd; I shall not want.

✠ He maketh me to lie down in green pastures: he leadeth me beside the still waters.

He restoreth my soul: he leadeth me in the paths of righteousness for his name's sake.

✠ Yea, though I walk through the valley of the shadow of death, I will fear no evil:

For thou *art* with me; thy rod and thy staff they comfort me.

✠ Thou preparest a table before me in the presence of mine enemies:

Thou anointest my head with oil; my cup runneth over.

✠ Surely goodness and mercy shall follow me all the days of my life: and I will dwell in the house of the LORD forever.

Psalm xxiii. 1–6.

One Hundred and Sixteenth Selection.

Strong Son of God, Immortal Love.

WHAT shall we then say to these things? If God *be* for us who *can be* against us?

✠ He that spared not his own Son, but delivered him up for us all, how shall he not with him also freely give us all things?

Who shall lay anything to the charge of God's elect? *It is* God that justifieth. Who *is* he that condemneth?

✠ *It is* Christ that died, yea rather, that is risen again, who is even at the right hand of God, who also maketh intercession for us.

Who shall separate us from the love of Christ? *shall* tribulation, or distress, or persecution, or famine, or nakedness, or peril, or sword?

✠ As it is written, For thy sake we are

killed all the day long; we are accounted as sheep for the slaughter.

Nay, in all these things we are more than conquerors through him that loved us. For I am persuaded, that neither death, nor life, nor angels, nor principalities, nor powers, nor things present, nor things to come,

✢ Nor height, nor depth, nor any other creature, shall be able to separate us from the love of God, which is in Christ Jesus our Lord.

Now unto him that is able to do exceeding abundantly above all that we ask or think, according to the power that worketh in us,

✢ Unto him *be* glory in the church by Christ Jesus throughout all ages, world without end. Amen.
Romans viii. 31-39; *Ephesians* iii. 20-21.

One Hundred and Seventeenth Selection.

Trials and Consolations.

MANY a time have they afflicted me from my youth, may Israel now say:

✠ Many a time have they afflicted me from my youth: yet they have not prevailed against me.

The ploughers ploughed upon my back: they made long their furrows.

✠ The LORD *is* righteous: he hath cut asunder the cords of the wicked.

Let them all be confounded and turned back that hate Zion.

✠ Let them be as the grass *upon* the housetops, which withereth afore it groweth up:

Wherewith the mower filleth not his hand; nor he that bindeth sheaves his bosom.

✠ Neither do they which go by say, The blessing of the LORD *be* upon you: we bless you in the name of the LORD.

When the LORD turned again the captivity of Zion, we were like them that dream.

✠ Then was our mouth filled with laughter, and our tongue with singing: then said they among the heathen, The LORD hath done great things for them.

The LORD hath done great things for us; *whereof* we are glad.

✠ Turn again our captivity, O Lord, as the streams in the south.

They that sow in tears shall reap in joy.

✠ He that goeth forth and weepeth, bearing precious seed, shall doubtless come again rejoicing, bringing his sheaves *with him*.

Psalm cxxix., cxxvi.

One Hundred and Eighteenth Selection.

Be Mindful of His Covenant.

GIVE thanks unto the Lord, call upon his name, make known his deeds among the people.

✠ Sing unto him, sing psalms unto him, talk ye of all his wondrous works.

Glory ye in his holy name: let the heart of them rejoice that seek the Lord.

✠ Seek the Lord and his strength, seek his face continually.

Remember his marvellous works that he hath done, his wonders, and the judgments of his mouth;

✠ O ye seed of Israel his servant, ye children of Jacob, his chosen ones.

§ 119   *The Joy of Religion.*   187

He *is* the LORD our God; his judgments *are* in all the earth.

✠ Be ye mindful always of his covenant; the word *which* he commanded to a thousand generations.

1 *Chronicles* xvi. 8-15.

One Hundred and Nineteenth Selection.

Fear not, O Land.

FEAR not, O land; be glad and rejoice:
✠ For the LORD will do great things.

Be not afraid, ye beasts of the field: for the pastures of the wilderness do spring, for the tree beareth her fruit, the fig-tree and the vine do yield their strength.

✠ Be glad then, ye children of Zion, and rejoice in the LORD your God:

For he hath given you the former rain moderately, and he will cause to come down for you the rain, the former rain, and the latter rain in the first *month*.

✠ And the floors shall be full of wheat, and the fats shall overflow with wine and oil.

And I will restore to you the years that the locust hath eaten, the canker-worm, and the caterpillar, and the palmer-worm, my great army which I sent among you.

✠ And ye shall eat in plenty, and be satisfied, and praise the name of the LORD your God, that hath dealt wondrously with you: and my people shall never be ashamed.

And ye shall know that I *am* in the midst of Israel, and *that* I *am* the LORD your God, and none else: and my people shall never be ashamed.

Joel ii. 21–27.

One Hundred and Twentieth Selection.

Therefore My Heart is Glad.

PRESERVE me, O God: for in thee do I put my trust.

✠ *O my soul*, thou hast said unto the LORD, thou *art* my LORD:

My goodness *extendeth* not to thee; *but* to the saints that *are* in the earth, and *to* the excellent, in whom *is* all my delight.

✠ Their sorrows shall be multiplied *that* hasten *after* another *god:*

Their drink offerings of blood will I not offer, nor take up their names into my lips.

✥ The Lord *is* the portion of mine inheritance and of my cup: thou maintainest my lot.

The lines are fallen unto me in pleasant *places;* yea, I have a goodly heritage.

✥ I will bless the Lord, who hath given me counsel: my reins also instruct me in the night seasons.

I have set the Lord always before me: because *he is* at my right hand, I shall not be moved.

✥ Therefore my heart is glad, and my glory rejoiceth: my flesh also shall rest in hope.

For thou wilt not leave my soul in hell; neither wilt thou suffer thine Holy One to see corruption.

✥ Thou wilt shew me the path of life: in thy presence *is* fullness of joy; at thy right hand *there are* pleasures for evermore.

Psalm xvi. 1-11.

One Hundred and Twenty-first Selection.

A New Name.

FOR Zion's sake will I not hold my peace, and for Jerusalem's sake I will not rest, until the righteousness thereof go forth as brightness, and the salvation thereof as a lamp *that* burneth.

✢ And the Gentiles shall see thy righteousness, and all kings thy glory:

And thou shalt be called by a new name, which the mouth of the LORD shall name.

✢ Thou shalt also be a crown of glory in the hand of the LORD, and a royal diadem in the hand of thy God.

Thou shalt no more be termed Forsaken; neither shall thy land any more be termed Desolate: but thou shalt be called Hephzibah, and thy land Beulah: for the LORD delighteth in thee, and thy land shall be married.

✢ Go through, go through the gates; prepare ye the way of the people;

Cast up, cast up the highway; gather out the stones; lift up a standard for the people.

✠ Behold, the LORD hath proclaimed unto the end of the world, Say ye to the daughter of Zion, Behold, thy salvation cometh;

Behold, his reward *is* with him, and his work before him.

✠ And they shall call them, The holy people, The redeemed of the LORD:

And thou shalt be called, Sought out, A city not forsaken. *Isaiah* lxii. 1-4; 10-12.

One Hundred and Twenty-second Selection.

Rejoice in the Lord.

REJOICE in the Lord alway: *and* again I say, Rejoice.

✠ Let your moderation be known unto all men. The Lord *is* at hand.

Be careful for nothing; but in every thing by prayer and supplication with thanksgiving let your requests be made known unto God.

✠ And the peace of God which passeth all understanding, shall keep your hearts and minds through Christ Jesus.

Finally, brethren, whatsoever things are true, whatsoever things *are* honest, whatsoever things *are* just, whatsoever things *are* pure, whatsoever things *are* lovely, whatsoever things *are* of good report;

✙ If *there be* any virtue, and if *there be* any praise, think on these things.

Philippians iv. 4–8.

One Hundred and Twenty-third Selection.

The Righteous shall Flourish.

*I*T is a good thing to give thanks unto the LORD, and to sing praises unto thy name, O Most High:

✙ To shew forth thy lovingkindness in the morning, and thy faithfulness every night,

Upon an instrument of ten strings, and upon the psaltery; upon the harp with a solemn sound.

✙ For thou, LORD, hast made me glad through thy work: I will triumph in the works of thy hands.

O LORD, how great are thy works! *and* thy thoughts are very deep.

✢ A brutish man knoweth not; neither doth a fool understand this.

When the wicked spring as the grass, and when all the workers of iniquity do flourish; *it is* that they shall be destroyed for ever :

✢ But thou, Lord, *art most* high for evermore.

The righteous shall flourish like the palm tree: he shall grow like a cedar in Lebanon.

✢ Those that be planted in the house of the Lord shall flourish in the courts of our God.

They shall still bring forth fruit in old age; they shall be fat and flourishing;

✢ To shew that the Lord *is* upright: *he is* my rock, and *there is* no unrighteousness in him.   *Psalm* xcii. 1-8; 12-15.

One Hundred and Twenty-fourth Selection.

We Believe and therefore Speak.

WE having the same spirit of faith, according as it is written, I believed, and therefore have I spoken; we also believe, and therefore speak;

✚ Knowing that he which raised up the Lord Jesus shall raise up us also by Jesus, and shall present *us* with you.

For all things *are* for your sakes, that the abundant grace might through the thanksgiving of many redound to the glory of God.

✚ For which cause we faint not; but though our outward man perish, yet the inward *man* is renewed day by day.

For our light affliction, which is but for a moment, worketh for us a far more exceeding *and* eternal weight of glory; while we look not at the things which are seen, but at the things which are not seen:

✚ For the things which are seen *are* temporal; but the things which are not seen *are* eternal.

Now unto him that is able to keep you from falling, and to present *you* faultless before the presence of his glory with exceeding joy,

✚ To the only wise God our Saviour, *be* glory and majesty, dominion and power, both now and ever. Amen.

2 *Corinthians* iv. 13–18; *Jude* 24, 25.

One Hundred and Twenty-fifth Selection.

Peace with God.

THEREFORE being justified by faith, we have peace with God through our Lord Jesus Christ:

✢ By whom also we have access by faith into this grace wherein we stand, and rejoice in hope of the glory of God.

And not only *so*, but we glory in tribulations also: knowing that tribulation worketh patience;

✢ And patience, experience; and experience, hope:

And hope maketh not ashamed; because the love of God is shed abroad in our hearts by the Holy Ghost which is given unto us.

✢ For when we were yet without strength, in due time Christ died for the ungodly.

For scarcely for a righteous man will one die:

✢ Yet peradventure for a good man some would even dare to die.

But God commendeth his love toward us,

in that, while we were yet sinners, Christ died for us.

✝ Much more then, being now justified by his blood, we shall be saved from wrath through him.

For if, when we were enemies, we were reconciled to God by the death of his Son;

✝ Much more, being reconciled, we shall be saved by his life.

And not only *so*, but we also joy in God through our Lord Jesus Christ, by whom we have now received the atonement.

Romans v. 1-11.

One Hundred and Twenty-sixth Selection.

Blessed are They that Dwell in Thy House.

HOW amiable *are* thy tabernacles, O LORD of hosts!

✝ My soul longeth, yea, even fainteth for the courts of the LORD: my heart and my flesh crieth out for the living God.

Yea, the sparrow hath found an house, and the swallow a nest for herself, where she may lay her young, *even* thine altars, O LORD of hosts, my King, and my God.

§ 126. *The Joy of Religion.*

✠ Blessed *are* they that dwell in thy house: they will be still praising thee.

Blessed *is* the man whose strength *is* in thee; in whose heart *are* the ways *of them*.

✠ *Who* passing through the valley of Baca make it a well; the rain also filleth the pools.

They go from strength to strength, *every one of them* in Zion appeareth before God.

✠ O Lord God of hosts, hear my prayer: give ear, O God of Jacob.

Behold, O God our shield, and look upon the face of thine anointed.

✠ For a day in thy courts *is* better than a thousand. I had rather be a door-keeper in the house of my God, than to dwell in the tents of wickedness.

For the Lord God *is* a sun and shield: the Lord will give grace and glory: no good *thing* will he withhold from them that walk uprightly.

✠ O Lord of hosts, blessed *is* the man that trusteth in thee.

Psalm lxxxiv. 1-12.

XV.

TRUST AND CONFIDENCE.

One Hundred and Twenty-seventh Selection.

God Our Refuge.

GOD *is* our refuge and strength, a very present help in trouble.

✢ Therefore will not we fear, though the earth be removed, and though the mountains be carried into the midst of the sea;

Though the waters thereof roar *and* be troubled, *though* the mountains shake with the swelling thereof.

✢ *There is* a river, the streams whereof shall make glad the city of God, the holy *place* of the tabernacles of the most High.

God *is* in the midst of her; she shall not be moved: God shall help her, *and that* right early.

✢ The heathen raged, the kingdoms

were moved: he uttered his voice, the earth melted.

The LORD of hosts *is* with us; the God of Jacob *is* our refuge.

☧ Come, behold the works of the LORD, what desolations he hath made in the earth.

He maketh wars to cease unto the end of the earth;

☧ He breaketh the bow, and cutteth the spear in sunder; he burneth the chariot in the fire.

Be still, and know that I *am* God: I will be exalted among the heathen, I will be exalted in the earth.

☧ The LORD of hosts *is* with us; the God of Jacob *is* our refuge. *Psalm* xlvi. 1-11.

One Hundred and Twenty-eighth Selection.

As the Mountains are round about Jerusalem.

THEY that trust in the LORD *shall be* as mount Zion, *which* cannot be removed, *but* abideth for ever.

☧ *As* the mountains *are* round about

Jerusalem, so the LORD *is* round about his people from henceforth even for ever.

For the rod of the wicked shall not rest upon the lot of the righteous; lest the righteous put forth their hands unto iniquity.

✠ Do good, O LORD, unto *those that be* good, and to *them that are* upright in their hearts.

As for such as turn aside unto their crooked ways, the LORD shall lead them forth with the workers of iniquity: *but* peace *shall be* upon Israel.

✠ The LORD reigneth, he is clothed with majesty;

The LORD is clothed with strength, *wherewith* he hath girded himself: the world also is established, that it cannot be moved.

✠ Thy throne *is* established of old: thou *art* from everlasting.

The floods have lifted up, O LORD, the floods have lifted up their voice; the floods lift up their waves.

✠ The LORD on high *is* mightier than the noise of many waters, *yea, than* the mighty waves of the sea.

Thy testimonies are very sure: holiness becometh thine house, O Lord, for ever.

Psalm cxxv. 1–5; xciii. 1–5.

One Hundred and Twenty-ninth Selection.

Be Thou My Strong Rock.

IN thee, O Lord, do I put my trust; let me never be ashamed: deliver me in thy righteousness.

✠ Bow down thine ear to me; deliver me speedily: be thou my strong rock, for an house of defence to save me.

For thou *art* my rock and my fortress; therefore for thy name's sake lead me, and guide me.

✠ Pull me out of the net that they have laid privily for me: for thou *art* my strength.

Into thine hand I commit my spirit: thou hast redeemed me, O Lord God of truth.

✠ I have hated them that regard lying vanities: but I trust in the Lord.

I will be glad and rejoice in thy mercy: for thou hast considered my trouble; thou hast known my soul in adversities;

✠ And hast not shut me up into the hand of the enemy: thou hast set my feet in a large room.

Oh how great *is* thy goodness, which thou hast laid up for them that fear thee; *which* thou hast wrought for them that trust in thee before the sons of men!

✠ Thou shalt hide them in the secret of thy presence from the pride of man: thou shalt keep them secretly in a pavilion from the strife of tongues.

Blessed *be* the LORD: for he hath shewed me his marvellous kindness in a strong city.

✠ For I said in my haste, I am cut off from before thine eyes: nevertheless thou heardest the voice of my supplications when I cried unto thee.

O love the LORD, all ye his saints: *for* the LORD preserveth the faithful, and plentifully rewardeth the proud doer.

✠ Be of good courage, and he shall strengthen your heart, all ye that hope in the LORD.

Psalm xxxi. 1-3; 19-24.

One Hundred and Thirtieth Selection.

A Shield to all that Trust Thee.

AS *for* God, his way *is* perfect: the word of the LORD is tried:

✢ He *is* a buckler to all those that trust in him.

For who *is* God save the LORD? or who *is* a rock save our God?

✢ *It is* God that girdeth me with strength, and maketh my way perfect.

He maketh my feet like hinds' *feet*, and setteth me upon my high places.

✢ He teacheth my hands to war, so that a bow of steel is broken by mine arms.

Thou hast also given me the shield of thy salvation: and thy right hand hath holden me up, and thy gentleness hath made me great.

✢ Thou hast enlarged my steps under me, that my feet did not slip.

The LORD liveth; and blessed *be* my Rock; and let the God of my salvation be exalted.

✢ *It is* God that avengeth me, and subdueth the people under me.

He delivereth me from mine enemies: yea, thou liftest me up above those that rise up against me: thou hast delivered me from the violent man.

✠ Therefore will I give thanks unto thee, O Lord, among the heathen, and sing praises unto thy name.

Great deliverance giveth he to his king; and sheweth mercy to his anointed, to David, and to his seed for evermore.

Psalm xviii. 30–36, 46–50.

One Hundred and Thirty-first Selection.

Preserve My Soul.

BOW down thine ear, O Lord, hear me: for I *am* poor and needy. Preserve my soul; for I *am* holy:

✠ O thou my God, save thy servant that trusteth in thee.

Be merciful unto me, O Lord? for I cry unto thee daily.

✠ Rejoice the soul of thy servant: for unto thee, O Lord, do I lift up my soul.

For thou, Lord, *art* good, and ready to

forgive; and plenteous in mercy unto all them that call upon thee.

✠ Give ear, O Lord, unto my prayer; and attend to the voice of my supplications.

In the day of my trouble I will call upon thee: for thou wilt answer me.

✠ Among the gods *there is* none like unto thee, O Lord; neither *are there any works* like unto thy works.

All nations whom thou hast made shall come and worship before thee, O Lord; and shall glorify thy name.

✠ For thou *art* great, and doest wondrous things: thou *art* God alone.

Teach me thy way, O Lord; I will walk in thy truth: unite my heart to fear thy name.

✠ I will praise thee, O Lord my God, with all my heart: and I will glorify thy name for evermore.

Psalm lxxxvi. 1-12.

One Hundred and Thirty-second Selection.

The Lord is on Our Side.

UNTO thee lift I up mine eyes, O thou that dwellest in the heavens.

✠ Behold, as the eyes of servants *look* unto the hand of their masters, *and* as the eyes of a maiden unto the hand of her mistress;

So our eyes *wait* upon the LORD our God, until that he have mercy upon us.

✠ Have mercy upon us, O LORD, have mercy upon us: for we are exceedingly filled with contempt.

Our soul is exceedingly filled with the scorning of those that are at ease, *and* with the contempt of the proud.

✠ If *it had* not *been* the LORD who was on our side, now may Israel say;

If *it had* not *been* the LORD who was on our side, when men rose up against us:

✠ Then they had swallowed us up quick, when their wrath was kindled against us:

Then the waters had overwhelmed us, the stream had gone over our soul:

✠ Then the proud waters had gone over our soul.

Blessed *be* the LORD, who hath not given us *as* a prey to their teeth.

✠ Our soul is escaped as a bird out of the snare of the fowlers: the snare is broken, and we are escaped.

Our help *is* in the name of the LORD, who made heaven and earth.

Psalm cxxiii.–cxxiv.

One Hundred and Thirty-third Selection.

I Waited Patiently for the Lord.

I WAITED patiently for the LORD; and he inclined unto me, and heard my cry. He brought me up also out of an horrible pit, out of the miry clay, and set my feet upon a rock, *and* established my goings.

✠ And he hath put a new song in my mouth, *even* praise unto our God: many shall see *it*, and fear, and shall trust in the LORD.

Blessed *is* that man that maketh the LORD his trust, and respecteth not the proud, nor such as turn aside to lies.

✠ Many, O LORD my God, *are* thy wonderful works *which* thou hast done, and thy thoughts *which are* to us-ward:

They cannot be reckoned up in order unto thee: *if* I would declare and speak *of them*, they are more than can be numbered.

✠ Sacrifice and offering thou didst not desire; mine ears hast thou opened: burnt offering and sin offering hast thou not required.

Then said I, Lo, I come: in the volume of the book *it is* written of me,

✠ I delight to do thy will, O my God: yea thy law *is* within my heart.

I have preached righteousness in the great congregation: lo, I have not refrained my lips, O LORD, thou knowest.

✠ I have not hid thy righteousness within my heart; I have declared thy faithfulness and thy salvation:

I have not concealed thy loving-kindness and thy truth from the great congregation.

✠ Withhold not thou thy tender mercies from me, O LORD: let thy loving-kindness and thy truth continually preserve me.

Psalm xl. 1-11.

One Hundred and Thirty-fourth Selection.

I have Trusted in Thy Mercy.

HOW long wilt thou forget me, O Lord? for ever? how long wilt thou hide thy face from me?

✠ How long shall I take counsel in my soul, *having* sorrow in my heart daily? how long shall mine enemy be exalted over me?

Consider *and* hear me, O Lord my God: lighten mine eyes, lest I sleep the *sleep of* death;

✠ Lest mine enemy say, I have prevailed against him; *and* those that trouble me rejoice when I am moved.

But I have trusted in thy mercy; my heart shall rejoice in thy salvation.

✠ I will sing unto the Lord, because he hath dealt bountifully with me.

The Lord hear thee in the day of trouble; the name of the God of Jacob defend thee;

✠ Send thee help from the sanctuary, and strengthen thee out of Zion;

Remember all thy offerings, and accept thy burnt sacrifice;

✢ Grant thee according to thine own heart, and fulfil all thy counsel.

We will rejoice in thy salvation, and in the name of our God we will set up *our* banners: the LORD fulfil all thy petitions.

✢ Now know I that the LORD saveth his anointed; he will hear him from his holy heaven with the saving strength of his right hand.

Some *trust* in chariots, and some in horses: but we will remember the name of the LORD our God.

✢ They are brought down and fallen: but we are risen, and stand upright.

Save, LORD: let the king hear us when we call.

Psalms xiii. 1-6; xx. 1-9.

One Hundred and Thirty-fifth Selection.

Thou Knewest My Path.

I CRIED unto the LORD with my voice; with my voice unto the LORD did I make my supplication.

✠ I poured out my complaint before him; I shewed before him my trouble.

When my spirit was overwhelmed within me, then thou knewest my path. In the way wherein I walked have they privily laid a snare for me.

✠ I looked on *my* right hand, and beheld, but *there was* no man that would know me: refuge failed me; no man cared for my soul.

I cried unto thee, O LORD: I said, Thou *art* my refuge *and* my portion in the land of the living.

✠ Attend unto my cry; for I am brought very low: deliver me from my persecutors; for they are stronger than I.

Bring my soul out of prison, that I may praise thy name:

✠ The righteous shall compass me about; for thou shalt deal bountifully with me.

Psalm cxlii. 1–7.

One Hundred and Thirty=sixth Selection.

In His Favour is Life.

I WILL extol thee, O LORD; for thou hast lifted me up, and hast not made my foes to rejoice over me.

✣ O Lord my God, I cried unto thee, and thou hast healed me.

O Lord, thou hast brought up my soul from the grave: thou hast kept me alive, that I should not go down to the pit.

✣ Sing unto the Lord, O ye saints of his, and give thanks at the remembrance of his holiness.

For his anger *endureth but* a moment; in his favour *is* life:

✣ Weeping may endure for a night, but joy *cometh* in the morning.

And in my prosperity I said, I shall never be moved.

✣ Lord, by thy favour thou hast made my mountain to stand strong:

Thou didst hide thy face, *and* I was troubled.

✣ I cried to thee, O Lord; and unto the Lord I made supplication.

What profit *is there* in my blood, when I go down to the pit? Shall the dust praise thee? shall it declare thy truth?

✣ Hear, O Lord, and have mercy upon me: Lord, be thou my helper.

Thou hast turned for me my mourning into dancing: thou hast put off my sackcloth, and girded me with gladness; to the end that *my* glory may sing praise to thee, and not be silent.

✟ O LORD my God, I will give thanks unto thee for ever. Psalm xxx. 1-12.

One Hundred and Thirty-seventh Selection.

Thou Makest Me Dwell in Safety.

HEAR me when I call, O God of my righteousness: thou hast enlarged me *when I was* in distress; have mercy upon me, and hear my prayer.

✟ O ye sons of men, how long *will ye turn* my glory into shame? *how long* will ye love vanity, *and* seek after leasing?

But know that the LORD hath set apart him that is godly for himself: the LORD will hear when I call unto him.

✟ Stand in awe, and sin not: commune with your own heart upon your bed, and be still.

Offer the sacrifices of righteousness, and put your trust in the LORD.

✟ *There be* many that say, Who will shew

us *any* good? LORD, lift thou up the light of thy countenance upon us.

Thou hast put gladness in my heart, more than in the time *that* their corn and their wine increased.

✢ I will both lay me down in peace, and sleep: for thou, LORD, only makest me dwell in safety.

Psalm iv. 1-8.

One Hundred and Thirty-eighth Selection.

Under the Shadow of the Almighty.

HE that dwelleth in the secret place of the most High shall abide under the shadow of the Almighty.

✢ I will say of the LORD, *He is* my refuge and my fortress: my God; in him will I trust.

Surely he shall deliver thee from the snare of the fowler, *and* from the noisome pestilence.

✢ He shall cover thee with his feathers, and under his wings shalt thou trust: his truth *shall be thy* shield and buckler. ·

Thou shalt not be afraid for the terror

by night; *nor* for the arrow *that* flieth by day;

✠ *Nor* for the pestilence *that* walketh in darkness; *nor* for the destruction *that* wasteth at noonday.

A thousand shall fall at thy side, and ten thousand at thy right hand; *but* it shall not come nigh thee.

✠ Only with thine eyes shalt thou behold and see the reward of the wicked.

Because thou hast made the LORD *which is* my refuge, *even* the most High, thy habitation;

✠ There shall no evil befall thee, neither shall any plague come nigh thy dwelling.

For he shall give his angels charge over thee, to keep thee in all thy ways.

✠ They shall bear thee up in their hands, lest thou dash thy foot against a stone.

Thou shalt tread upon the lion and adder: the young lion and the dragon shalt thou trample under feet.

✠ Because he hath set his love upon me, therefore will I deliver him: I will set him on high, because he hath known my name.

He shall call upon me, and I will answer

him; I *will be* with him in trouble; I will deliver him, and honour him.

✠ With long life will I satisfy him, and shew him my salvation.

Psalm xci. 1-16.

One Hundred and Thirty-ninth Selection.

The Rock that is Higher than I.

HEAR my cry, O God; attend unto my prayer.

✠ From the end of the earth will I cry unto thee, when my heart is overwhelmed: lead me to the rock *that* is higher than I.

For thou hast been a shelter for me, *and* a strong tower from the enemy.

✠ I will abide in thy tabernacle for ever: I will trust in the covert of thy wings.

For thou, O God, hast heard my vows: thou hast given *me* the heritage of those that fear thy name.

✠ Thou wilt prolong the king's life: *and* his years as many generations.

He shall abide before God for ever: O prepare mercy and truth, *which* may preserve him.

✠ So will I sing praise unto thy name for ever, that I may daily perform my vows.

Psalm lxi. 1–8.

One Hundred and Fortieth Selection.

I shall not be Moved.

TRULY my soul waiteth upon God: from him *cometh* my salvation.

✠ He only *is* my rock and my salvation; *he is* my defence; I shall not be greatly moved.

How long will ye imagine mischief against a man? ye shall be slain all of you: as a bowing wall *shall ye be, and as* a tottering fence.

✠ They only consult to cast *him* down from his excellency: they delight in lies: they bless with their mouth, but they curse inwardly.

My soul, wait thou only upon God; for my expectation *is* from him.

✠ He only *is* my rock and my salvation: *he is* my defence; I shall not be moved.

In God *is* my salvation and my glory: the rock of my strength, *and* my refuge, *is* in God.

✛ Trust in him at all times; ye people, pour out your heart before him: God *is* a refuge for us.

Surely men of low degree *are* vanity, *and* men of high degree *are* a lie: to be laid in the balance, they *are* altogether *lighter* than vanity.

✛ Trust not in oppression, and become not vain in robbery: if riches increase, set not your heart *upon them.*

God hath spoken once: twice have I heard this; that power *belongeth* unto God.

✛ Also unto thee, O Lord, *belongeth* mercy: for thou renderest to every man according to his work.

Psalm lxii. 1-12.

One Hundred and Forty=first Selection.

The Lord is Thy Keeper.

I WILL lift up mine eyes unto the hills, from whence cometh my help.

✛ My help *cometh* from the Lord, which made heaven and earth.

He will not suffer thy foot to be moved: he that keepeth thee will not slumber.

✠ The LORD *is* thy keeper: the LORD *is* thy shade upon thy right hand.

The sun shall not smite thee by day, nor the moon by night.

✠ The LORD shall preserve thee from all evil: he shall preserve thy soul.

The LORD shall preserve thy going out and thy coming in from this time forth, and even for evermore.

Psalm cxxi. 1–8.

One Hundred and Forty-second Selection.

Is not God in the Height of Heaven?

IS not God in the height of heaven? and behold the height of the stars, how high they are!

✠ And thou sayest, How doth God know? can he judge through the dark cloud?

Thick clouds *are* a covering to him, that he seeth not; and he walketh in the circuit of heaven.

✠ Hast thou marked the old way which wicked men have trodden?

Which were cut down out of time, whose foundation was overflown with a flood:

✢ Which said unto God, Depart from us: and what can the Almighty do for them?

Yet he filled their houses with good *things:* but the counsel of the wicked is far from me.

✢ The righteous see *it*, and are glad: and the innocent laugh them to scorn.

Whereas our substance is not cut down, but the remnant of them the fire consumeth.

✢ Acquaint now thyself with him, and be at peace: thereby good shall come unto thee.

Receive, I pray thee, the law from his mouth, and lay up his words in thine heart.

✢ If thou return to the Almighty, thou shalt be built up, thou shalt put away iniquity far from thy tabernacles.

Then shalt thou lay up gold as dust, and the *gold* of Ophir as the stones of the brooks.

✢ Yea, the Almighty shall be thy defence, and thou shalt have plenty of silver.

For then shalt thou have thy delight in

the Almighty, and shalt lift up thy face unto God.

✠ Thou shalt make thy prayer unto him, and he shall hear thee, and thou shalt pay thy vows.

Thou shalt also decree a thing, and it shall be established unto thee: and the light shall shine upon thy ways.

✠ When *men* are cast down, then thou shalt say, *There is* lifting up; and he shall save the humble person.

He shall deliver the island of the innocent: and it is delivered by the pureness of thine hands.

Job xxii. 12-30.

One Hundred and Forty-third Selection.

He Beholdeth all the Sons of Men.

THE LORD looketh from heaven; he beholdeth all the sons of men.

✠ From the place of his habitation he looketh upon all the inhabitants of the earth.

He fashioneth their hearts alike; he considereth all their works.

✠ There is no king saved by the multitude of an host: a mighty man is not delivered by much strength.

An horse *is* a vain thing for safety: neither shall he deliver *any* by his great strength.

✠ Behold, the eye of the LORD *is* upon them that fear him, upon them that hope in his mercy;

To deliver their soul from death, and to keep them alive in famine.

✠ Our soul waiteth for the LORD: he *is* our help and our shield.

For our heart shall rejoice in him, because we have trusted in his holy name.

✠ Let thy mercy, O LORD, be upon us, according as we hope in thee.

Psalm xxxiii. 13-22.

One Hundred and Forty-fourth Selection.

A Prayer in Trouble.

HEAR my prayer, O LORD, and let my cry come unto thee.

✠ Hide not thy face from me in the day *when* I am in trouble; incline thine ear unto me: in the day *when* I call, answer me speedily.

When the Lord shall build up Zion, he shall appear in his glory.

✙ He will regard the prayer of the destitute, and not despise their prayer.

This shall be written for the generation to come: and the people which shall be created shall praise the Lord.

✙ For he hath looked down from the height of his sanctuary; from heaven did the Lord behold the earth;

To hear the groaning of the prisoner; to loose those that are appointed to death;

✙ To declare the name of the Lord in Zion, and his praise in Jerusalem;

When the people are gathered together, and the kingdoms, to serve the Lord.

✙ He weakened my strength in the way; he shortened my days.

I said, O my God, take me not away in the midst of my days: thy years *are* throughout all generations.

✙ Of old hast thou laid the foundation of the earth: and the heavens *are* the work of thy hands.

They shall perish, but thou shalt endure:

yea, all of them shall wax old like a garment; as a vesture shalt thou change them, and they shall be changed:

✢ But thou *art* the same, and thy years shall have no end.

The children of thy servants shall continue, and their seed shall be established before thee.

Psalm cii. 1-2, 16-28.

One Hundred and Forty-fifth Selection.

My Fortress and My Deliverer.

I WILL love thee, O LORD, my strength.
✢ The LORD *is* my rock, and my fortress, and my deliverer; my God, my strength, in whom I will trust;

My buckler, and the horn of my salvation, *and* my high tower.

✢ I will call upon the LORD, *who is worthy* to be praised: so shall I be saved from mine enemies.

The LORD rewarded me according to my righteousness; according to the cleanness of my hands hath he recompensed me.

✢ For I have kept the ways of the Lord, and have not wickedly departed from my God.

For all his judgments *were* before me, and I did not put away his statutes from me.

✢ I was also upright before him, and I kept myself from mine iniquity.

Therefore hath the Lord recompensed me according to my righteousness, according to the cleanness of my hands in his eyesight.

✢ With the merciful thou wilt shew thyself merciful; with an upright man thou wilt shew thyself upright;

With the pure thou wilt shew thyself pure; and with the froward thou wilt shew thyself froward.

✢ For thou wilt save the afflicted people; but wilt bring down high looks.

For thou wilt light my candle: the Lord my God will enlighten my darkness.

Psalm xviii. 1-3, 20-28.

One Hundred and Forty-sixth Selection.

Happy is that People Whose God is the Lord.

BLESSED *be* the Lord my strength, which teacheth my hands to war, *and* my fingers to fight:

✢ My goodness, and my fortress; my high tower, and my deliverer; my shield, and *he* in whom I trust; who subdueth my people under me.

Lord, what *is* man, that thou takest knowledge of him! *or* the son of man, that thou makest account of him!

✢ Man is like to vanity: his days *are* as a shadow that passeth away.

Bow thy heavens, O Lord, and come down: touch the mountains, and they shall smoke.

✢ Cast forth lightning, and scatter them: shoot out thine arrows, and destroy them.

Send thine hand from above; rid me, and deliver me out of great waters, from the hand of strange children;

✢ Whose mouth speaketh vanity, and

their right hand *is* a right hand of falsehood.

I will sing a new song unto thee, O God: upon a psaltery *and* an instrument of ten strings will I sing praises unto thee.

✣ *It is he* that giveth salvation unto kings: who delivereth David his servant from the hurtful sword.

Rid me, and deliver me from the hand of strange children, whose mouth speaketh vanity, and their right hand *is* a right hand of falsehood:

✣ That our sons *may be* as plants grown up in their youth; *that* our daughters *may be* as corner stones, polished *after* the similitude of a palace:

That our garners *may be* full, affording all manner of store; *that* our sheep may bring forth thousands and ten thousands in our streets:

✣ *That* our oxen *may be* strong to labour; *that there be* no breaking in, nor going out; that *there be* no complaining in our streets.

Happy *is that* people, that is in such a case: *yea*, happy *is that* people, whose God *is* the LORD.

Psalm cxliv. 1–15.

XVI.

COURAGE AND HOPE.

One Hundred and Forty-seventh Selection.

The Armour of God.

FINALLY, my brethren, be strong in the Lord, and in the power of his might.

✠ Put on the whole armour of God, that ye may be able to stand against the wiles of the devil.

For we wrestle not against flesh and blood, but against principalities, against powers, against the rulers of the darkness of this world, against spiritual wickedness in high *places*.

✠ Wherefore take unto you the whole armour of God, that ye may be able to withstand in the evil day, and having done all, to stand.

Stand therefore, having your loins girt about with truth, and having on the breastplate of righteousness;

✢ And your feet shod with the preparation of the gospel of peace;

Above all, taking the shield of faith, wherewith ye shall be able to quench all the fiery darts of the wicked.

✢ And take the helmet of salvation, and the sword of the Spirit, which is the word of God:

Praying always with all prayer and supplication in the Spirit, and watching thereunto with all perseverance and supplication for all saints.

Ephesians vi. 10-18.

One Hundred and Forty-eighth Selection.

Be of Good Courage.

THE LORD *is* my light and my salvation; whom shall I fear?

✢ The LORD *is* the strength of my life; of whom shall I be afraid?

When the wicked, *even* mine enemies and my foes, came upon me to eat up my flesh, they stumbled and fell.

✢ Though an host should encamp against me, my heart shall not fear: though war should rise against me, in this *will* I *be* confident.

One *thing* have I desired of the Lord, that will I seek after; that I may dwell in the house of the Lord all the days of my life, to behold the beauty of the Lord, and to enquire in his temple.

✢ For in the time of trouble he shall hide me in his pavilion: in the secret of his tabernacle shall he hide me; he shall set me up upon a rock.

And now shall mine head be lifted up above mine enemies round about me: therefore will I offer in his tabernacle sacrifices of joy;

✢ I will sing, yea, I will sing praises unto the Lord.

Hear, O Lord, *when* I cry with my voice: have mercy also upon me, and answer me.

✢ *When thou saidst*, Seek ye my face; my heart said unto thee, Thy face, Lord, will I seek.

Hide not thy face *far* from me; put not thy servant away in anger: thou hast been my help; leave me not, neither forsake me, O God of my salvation.

✢ When my father and my mother forsake me, then the LORD will take me up.

Teach me thy way, O LORD, and lead me in a plain path, because of mine enemies.

✢ Deliver me not over unto the will of mine enemies: for false witnesses are risen up against me, and such as breathe out cruelty.

I had fainted, unless I had believed to see the goodness of the LORD in the land of the living.

✢ Wait on the LORD: be of good courage, and he shall strengthen thine heart: wait, I say, on the LORD.

Psalm xxvii. 1-14.

One Hundred and Forty-ninth Selection.

Hope in God.

JUDGE me, O God, and plead my cause against an ungodly nation:

✢ O deliver me from the deceitful and unjust man.

For thou *art* the God of my strength: why dost thou cast me off? why go I mourning because of the oppression of the enemy?

✠ O send out thy light and thy truth: let them lead me; let them bring me unto thy holy hill, and to thy tabernacles.

Then will I go unto the altar of God, unto God my exceeding joy:

✠ Yea, upon the harp will I praise thee, O God my God.

Why art thou cast down, O my soul? and why art thou disquieted within me? hope in God:

✠ For I shall yet praise him *who is* the health of my countenance, and my God.

LORD, my heart is not haughty, nor mine eyes lofty:

✠ Neither do I exercise myself in great matters, or in things too high for me.

Surely I have behaved and quieted myself, as a child that is weaned of his mother: my soul *is* even as a weaned child.

✠ Let Israel hope in the LORD from henceforth and for ever.

Psalms xliii. 1-5; cxxxi. 1-3.

One Hundred and Fiftieth Selection.

Watch and Be Sober.

BUT of the times and the seasons, brethren, ye have no need that I write unto you.

✠ For yourselves know perfectly that the day of the Lord so cometh as a thief in the night.

For when they shall say, Peace and safety; then sudden destruction cometh upon them, as travail upon a woman with child; and they shall not escape.

✠ But ye, brethren, are not in darkness, that that day should overtake you as a thief.

Ye are all the children of light, and the children of the day: we are not of the night, nor of darkness.

✠ Therefore let us not sleep, as *do* others; but let us watch and be sober.

For they that sleep sleep in the night; and they that be drunken are drunken in the night.

✠ But let us, who are of the day, be sober, putting on the breastplate of faith and love; and for an helmet, the hope of salvation.

For God hath not appointed us to wrath, but to obtain salvation by our Lord Jesus Christ,

✠ Who died for us, that, whether we wake or sleep, we should live together with him.

1 *Thessalonians* v. 1–10.

One Hundred and Fifty-first Selection.

Always Confident.

THEREFORE *we are* always confident, knowing that, whilst we are at home in the body, we are absent from the Lord:

✠ (For we walk by faith, not by sight:)

We are confident, *I say*, and willing rather to be absent from the body, and to be present with the Lord.

✠ Wherefore we labour, that, whether present or absent, we may be accepted of him.

For the love of Christ constraineth us; because we thus judge, that if one died for all, then were all dead:

✢ And *that* he died for all, that they which live should not henceforth live unto themselves, but unto him which died for them, and rose again.

Wherefore henceforth know we no man after the flesh:

✢ Yea, though we have known Christ after the flesh, yet now henceforth know we *him* no more.

Therefore, if any man *be* in Christ, *he is* a new creature:

✢ Old things are passed away; behold, all things are become new.

And all things *are* of God, who hath reconciled us to himself by Jesus Christ,

✢ And hath given to us the ministry of reconciliation;

To wit, that God was in Christ, reconciling the world unto himself, not imputing their trespasses unto them;

✢ And hath committed unto us the word of reconciliation.

Now then we are ambassadors for Christ, as though God did beseech *you* by us: we pray *you* in Christ's stead, be ye reconciled to God.

✢ For he hath made him *to be* sin for

us, who knew no sin; that we might be made the righteousness of God in him.

2 Corinthians v. 6–9, 14–21.

One Hundred and Fifty-second Selection.

Let us Run with Patience.

WHEREFORE, seeing we also are compassed about with so great a cloud of witnesses, let us lay aside every weight, and the sin which doth so easily beset *us*,

✠ And let us run with patience the race that is set before us,

Looking unto Jesus the author and finisher of *our* faith;

✠ Who for the joy that was set before him endured the cross, despising the shame, and is set down at the right hand of the throne of God.

For consider him that endured such contradiction of sinners against himself, lest ye be wearied and faint in your minds.

✠ Ye have not yet resisted unto blood, striving against sin.

And ye have forgotten the exhortation which speaketh unto you as unto children, My son, despise not thou the chastening of the Lord, nor faint when thou art rebuked of him:

✠ For whom the Lord loveth he chasteneth, and scourgeth every son whom he receiveth.

Now no chastening for the present seemeth to be joyous, but grievous: nevertheless afterward it yieldeth the peaceable fruit of righteousness unto them which are exercised thereby.

✠ Wherefore lift up the hands which hang down, and the feeble knees;

And make straight paths for your feet, lest that which is lame be turned out of the way; but let it rather be healed.

✠ Follow peace with all *men*, and holiness, without which no man shall see the Lord.

Hebrews xii. 1–6, 11–14.

One Hundred and Fifty-third Selection.

Grace to Help in Time of Need.

THERE remaineth therefore a rest to the people of God. For he that is entered into his rest, he also hath ceased from his own works, as God *did* from his.

✠ Let us labour therefore to enter into that rest, lest any man fall after the same example of unbelief.

For the word of God *is* quick, and powerful, and sharper than any twoedged sword, piercing even to the dividing asunder of soul and spirit, and of the joints and marrow, and *is* a discerner of the thoughts and intents of the heart.

✠ Neither is there any creature that is not manifest in his sight: but all things *are* naked and opened unto the eyes of him with whom we have to do.

Seeing then that we have a great high priest, that is passed into the heavens, Jesus the Son of God,

✠ Let us hold fast *our* profession.

For we have not an high priest which cannot be touched with the feeling of our infirmities; but was in all points tempted like as *we are*, *yet* without sin.

✠ Let us therefore come boldly unto the throne of grace, that we may obtain mercy, and find grace to help in time of need.

Hebrews iv. 9-16.

One Hundred and Fifty-fourth Selection.

The New Covenant.

THIS *is* the covenant that I will make with them after those days, saith the Lord; I will put my laws into their hearts, and in their minds will I write them;

✠ And their sins and iniquities will I remember no more.

Now, where remission of these *is, there is* no more offering for sin.

✠ Having therefore, brethren, boldness to enter into the holiest by the blood of Jesus,

By a new and living way, which he hath consecrated for us, through the vail, that is to say, his flesh;

✠ And *having* an high priest over the house of God;

Let us draw near with a true heart, in full assurance of faith, having our hearts sprinkled from an evil conscience, and our bodies washed with pure water.

✢ Let us hold fast the profession of *our* faith without wavering; for he *is* faithful that promised:

And let us consider one another to provoke unto love, and to good works:

✢ Not forsaking the assembling of ourselves together, as the manner of some *is;*

But exhorting *one another;* and so much the more, as ye see the day approaching.

Hebrews x. 16–25.

One Hundred and Fifty-fifth Selection.

I shall yet Praise Him.

AS the hart panteth after the water brooks, so panteth my soul after thee, O God.

✢ My soul thirsteth for God, for the living God: when shall I come and appear before God?

My tears have been my meat day and

night, while they continually say unto me, Where *is* thy God?

✠ When I remember these *things*, I pour out my soul in me: for I had gone with the multitude, I went with them to the house of God, with the voice of joy and praise, with a multitude that kept holy-day.

Why art thou cast down, O my soul? and *why* art thou disquieted in me? hope thou in God: for I shall yet praise him *for* the help of his countenance.

✠ O my God, my soul is cast down within me: therefore will I remember thee from the land of Jordan, and of the Hermonites, from the hill Mizar.

Deep calleth unto deep at the noise of thy waterspouts: all thy waves and thy billows are gone over me.

✠ *Yet* the Lord will command his loving-kindness in the day-time, and in the night his song *shall be* with me, *and* my prayer unto the God of my life.

I will say unto God my rock, Why hast thou forgotten me? why go I mourning because of the oppression of the enemy?

✠ *As* with a sword in my bones, mine

enemies reproach me; while they say daily unto me, Where *is* thy God?

Why art thou cast down, O my soul? and why art thou disquieted within me? hope thou in God: for I shall yet praise him, *who is* the health of my countenance, and my God.

Psalm xlii. 1–11.

One Hundred and Fifty-sixth Selection.

Forget not the Lord.

ALL the commandments which I command thee this day shall ye observe to do, that ye may live, and multiply, and go in and possess the land which the LORD sware unto your fathers.

✠ Therefore thou shalt keep the commandments of the LORD thy God, to walk in his ways, and to fear him.

For the LORD thy God bringeth thee into a good land, a land of brooks of water, of fountains, and depths that spring out of valleys and hills;

✠ A land of wheat, and barley, and vines, and fig-trees, and pomegranates, a land of oil-olive, and honey;

A land wherein thou shalt eat bread without scarceness, thou shalt not lack any *thing* in it; a land whose stones *are* iron, and out of whose hills thou mayest dig brass.

✠ When thou hast eaten and art full, then thou shalt bless the Lord thy God for the good land which he hath given thee.

Beware that thou forget not the Lord thy God, in not keeping his commandments, and his judgments, and his statutes, which I command thee this day:

✠ Lest *when* thou hast eaten, and art full, and hast built goodly houses, and dwelt *therein;*

And *when* thy herds and thy flocks multiply, and thy silver and thy gold is multiplied, and all that thou hast is multiplied;

✠ Then thine heart be lifted up, and thou forget the Lord thy God, which brought thee forth out of the land of Egypt, from the house of bondage;

Who led thee through that great and terrible wilderness, *wherein were* fiery serpents, and scorpions, and drought, where *there was* no water:

✠ Who brought thee forth water out of the rock of flint;

Who fed thee in the wilderness with manna, which thy fathers knew not, that he might humble thee, and that he might prove thee, to do thee good at thy latter end:

✠ And thou say in thine heart, My power and the might of *mine* hand hath gotten me this wealth.

But thou shalt remember the LORD thy God: for *it is* he that giveth thee power to get wealth, that he may establish his covenant which he sware unto thy fathers, as *it is* this day.

Deuteronomy viii. 1, 6–18.

One Hundred and Fifty-seventh Selection.

Keep His Commandments.

THEREFORE thou shalt love the LORD thy God,

✠ And keep his charge, and his statutes, and his judgments, and his commandments, always.

And it shall come to pass, if ye shall

hearken diligently unto my commandments which I command you this day,

✠ To love the LORD your God, and to serve him with all your heart and with all your soul,

That I will give *you* the rain of your land in his due season, the first rain and the latter rain, that thou mayest gather in thy corn, and thy wine, and thine oil.

✠ And I will send grass in thy fields for thy cattle, that thou mayest eat and be full.

Take heed to yourselves, that your heart be not deceived, and ye turn aside, and serve other gods, and worship them;

✠ And *then* the LORD's wrath be kindled against you, and he shut up the heaven, that there be no rain, and that the land yield not her fruit;

And *lest* ye perish quickly from off the good land which the LORD giveth you.

✠ Therefore shall ye lay up these my words in your heart and in your soul,

And bind them for a sign upon your hand, that they may be as frontlets between your eyes.

✠ And ye shall teach them your children, speaking of them when thou sittest in thine house, and when thou walkest by the way, when thou liest down, and when thou risest up.

And thou shalt write them upon the door post of thine house, and upon thy gates:

✠ That your days may be multiplied, and the days of your children, in the land which the LORD sware unto your fathers to give them, as the days of heaven upon the earth.

Deuteronomy xi. 1, 13-21.

One Hundred and Fifty-eighth Selection.

The Blessings of Obedience.

AND it shall come to pass, if thou shalt hearken diligently unto the voice of the LORD thy God, to observe *and* to do all his commandments which I command thee this day:

✠ That the LORD thy God will set thee on high above all nations of the earth:

And all these blessings shall come on thee, and overtake thee, if thou shalt hearken unto the voice of the LORD thy God.

✠ Blessed *shalt* thou *be* in the city, and blessed *shalt* thou *be* in the field.

Blessed *shall be* the fruit of thy body, and the fruit of thy ground, and the fruit of thy cattle, the increase of thy kine, and the flocks of thy sheep.

✠ Blessed *shall be* thy basket and thy store.

Blessed *shalt* thou *be* when thou comest in, and blessed *shalt* thou *be* when thou goest out.

✠ The LORD shall cause thine enemies that rise up against thee to be smitten before thy face:

They shall come out against thee one way, and flee before thee seven ways.

✠ The LORD shall command the blessing upon thee in thy storehouses, and in all that thou settest thine hand unto:

And he shall bless thee in the land which the LORD thy God giveth thee.

✠ The LORD shall establish thee an holy people unto himself, as he hath sworn unto thee,

If thou shalt keep the commandments of the LORD thy God, and walk in his ways.

✠ And all people of the earth shall see that thou art called by the name of the LORD; and they shall be afraid of thee.

Deuteronomy xxviii. 1-10.

One Hundred and Fifty-ninth Selection.

A Vow of Service.

I WILL sing of mercy and judgment: unto thee, O LORD, will I sing.

✠ I will behave myself wisely in a perfect way. O when wilt thou come unto me? I will walk within my house with a perfect heart.

I will set no wicked thing before mine eyes: I hate the work of them that turn aside; *it* shall not cleave to me.

✠ A froward heart shall depart from me: I will not know a wicked *person*.

Whoso privily slandereth his neighbour, him will I cut off: him that hath an high look and a proud heart will not I suffer.

✠ Mine eyes *shall be* upon the faithful of the land, that they may dwell with me:

He that walketh in a perfect way, he shall serve me.

✠ He that worketh deceit shall not dwell

within my house: he that telleth lies shall not tarry in my sight.

I will early destroy all the wicked of the land; that I may cut off all wicked doers from the city of the LORD.
Psalm ci. 1–8.

One Hundred and Sixtieth Selection.

A Vow Performed and Rewarded.

LORD, remember David, *and* all his afflictions:

✠ How he sware unto the LORD, *and* vowed unto the mighty *God* of Jacob;

Surely I will not come into the tabernacle of my house, nor go up into my bed;

✠ I will not give sleep to mine eyes, *or* slumber to mine eyelids,

Until I find out a place for the LORD, an habitation for the mighty *God* of Jacob.

✠ Lo, we heard of it at Ephratah: we found it in the fields of the wood.

We will go into his tabernacles: we will worship at his footstool.

✠ Arise, O LORD, into thy rest; thou, and the ark of thy strength.

Let thy priests be clothed with righteousness; and let thy saints shout for joy.

✠ For thy servant David's sake turn not away the face of thine anointed.

The LORD hath sworn *in* truth unto David; he will not turn from it; Of the fruit of thy body will I set upon thy throne.

✠ If thy children will keep my covenant and my testimony that I shall teach them; their children also shall sit upon thy throne for evermore.

For the LORD hath chosen Zion; he hath desired *it* for his habitation.

✠ This *is* my rest for ever: here will I dwell; for I have desired it.

I will abundantly bless her provision: I will satisfy her poor with bread.

✠ I will also clothe her priests with salvation, and her saints shall shout aloud for joy.

There will I make the horn of David to bud: I have ordained a lamp for mine anointed.

✠ His enemies will I clothe with shame: but upon himself shall his crown flourish.

Psalm cxxxii. 1-18.

XVII.

SERVICE AND REWARD.

One Hundred and Sixty-first Selection.

Good Resolutions.

JUDGE me, O Lord; for I have walked in mine integrity: I have trusted also in the Lord; *therefore* I shall not slide.

✠ Examine me, O Lord, and prove me; try my reins and my heart.

For thy lovingkindness *is* before mine eyes: and I have walked in thy truth.

✠ I have not sat with vain persons, neither will I go in with dissemblers.

I have hated the congregation of evil doers; and will not sit with the wicked.

✠ I will wash mine hands in innocency: so will I compass thine altar, O Lord:

That I may publish with the voice of thanksgiving, and tell of all thy wondrous works.

✠ Lord, I have loved the habitation of

thy house, and the place where thine honour dwelleth.

Gather not my soul with sinners, nor my life with bloody men:

✠ In whose hands *is* mischief, and their right hand is full of bribes.

But as for me, I will walk in mine integrity: redeem me, and be merciful unto me.

✠ My foot standeth in an even place: in the congregations will I bless the Lord.

Psalm xxvi. 1-12.

One Hundred and Sixty-second Selection.

An Upright Character.

LORD, who shall abide in thy tabernacle? who shall dwell in thy holy hill?

✠ He that walketh uprightly, and worketh righteousness, and speaketh the truth in his heart.

He that backbiteth not with his tongue, nor doeth evil to his neighbour, nor taketh up a reproach against his neighbour.

✜ In whose eyes a vile person is contemned; but he honoureth them that fear the LORD.

He that sweareth to *his own* hurt, and changeth not. *He that* putteth not out his money to usury, nor taketh reward against the innocent.

✜ He that doeth these *things* shall never be moved.

Psalm xv. 1-5.

One Hundred and Sixty-third Selection.

Praise of a Good Life.

A GOOD name *is* rather to be chosen than great riches, *and* loving favour rather than silver and gold.

✜ The rich and poor meet together: the LORD *is* the maker of them all.

A prudent *man* foreseeth the evil, and hideth himself: but the simple pass on, and are punished.

✜ By humility *and* the fear of the LORD *are* riches, and honour, and life.

Thorns *and* snares *are* in the way of the froward: he that doth keep his soul shall be far from them.

✠ Train up a child in the way he should go: and when he is old, he will not depart from it.

The rich ruleth over the poor, and the borrower *is* servant to the lender.

✠ He that soweth iniquity shall reap vanity: and the rod of his anger shall fail.

He that hath a bountiful eye shall be blessed; for he giveth of his bread to the poor.

✠ Cast out the scorner, and contention shall go out; yea, strife and reproach shall cease.

He that loveth pureness of heart, *for* the grace of his lips the king *shall be* his friend.

✠ The eyes of the LORD preserve knowledge, and he overthroweth the words of the transgressor. *Proverbs* xxii. 1-12.

One Hundred and Sixty-fourth Selection.

The Reward of Righteousness.

THE LORD rewarded me according to my righteousness; according to the cleanness of my hands hath he recompensed me.

✠ For I have kept the ways of the LORD, and have not wickedly departed from my God.

For all his judgments *were* before me: and *as for* his statutes, I did not depart from them.

✠ I was also upright before him, and have kept myself from mine iniquity.

Therefore the LORD hath recompensed me according to my righteousness; according to my cleanness in his eyesight.

✠ With the merciful thou wilt shew thyself merciful, *and* with the upright man thou wilt shew thyself upright.

. With the pure thou wilt shew thyself pure; and with the froward thou wilt shew thyself unsavoury.

✠ And the afflicted people thou wilt save: but thine eyes *are* upon the haughty, *that* thou mayest bring *them* down.

For thou *art* my lamp, O LORD: and the LORD will lighten my darkness.

2 *Samuel* xxii. 21–29.

One Hundred and Sixty-fifth Selection.

The Two Paths.

ENTER not into the path of the wicked, and go not in the way of evil *men*.

✠ Avoid it, pass not by it, turn from it, and pass away.

For they sleep not, except they have done mischief; and their sleep is taken away, unless they cause *some* to fall.

✠ For they eat the bread of wickedness, and drink the wine of violence.

But the path of the just *is* as the shining light, that shineth more and more unto the perfect day.

✠ The way of the wicked *is* as darkness: they know not at what they stumble.

My son, attend to my words; incline thine ear unto my sayings.

✠ Let them not depart from thine eyes; keep them in the midst of thine heart.

For they *are* life unto those that find them, and health to all their flesh.

✠ Keep thy heart with all diligence; for out of it *are* the issues of life.

Put away from thee a froward mouth, and perverse lips put far from thee.

✠ Let thine eyes look right on, and let thine eyelids look straight before thee.

Ponder the path of thy feet, and let all thy ways be established.

✠ Turn not to the right hand nor to the left: remove thy foot from evil.

Proverbs iv. 14-27.

One Hundred and Sixty-sixth Selection.

Trust in the Lord and Do Good.

FRET not thyself because of evil doers, neither be thou envious against the workers of iniquity.

✠ For they shall soon be cut down like the grass, and wither as the green herb.

Trust in the LORD, and do good; *so* shalt thou dwell in the land, and verily thou shalt be fed.

✠ Delight thyself also in the LORD; and he shall give thee the desires of thine heart.

Commit thy way unto the LORD; trust also in him; and he shall bring *it* to pass.

✙ And he shall bring forth thy righteousness as the light, and thy judgment as the noonday.

Rest in the LORD, and wait patiently for him: fret not thyself because of him who prospereth in his way, because of the man who bringeth wicked devices to pass.

✙ Cease from anger, and forsake wrath: fret not thyself in any wise to do evil.

For evil doers shall be cut off: but those that wait upon the LORD, they shall inherit the earth.

✙ For yet a little while, and the wicked *shall* not *be:* yea, thou shalt diligently consider his place, and it *shall* not *be.*

But the meek shall inherit the earth; and shall delight themselves in the abundance of peace.

Psalm xxxvii. 1–11.

One Hundred and Sixty-seventh Selection.

The Happy Man.

BLESSED *is* the man that walketh not in the counsel of the ungodly, nor standeth in the way of sinners, nor sitteth in the seat of the scornful.

✠ But his delight *is* in the law of the LORD; and in his law doth he meditate day and night.

And he shall be like a tree planted by the rivers of water, that bringeth forth his fruit in his season; his leaf also shall not wither; and whatsoever he doeth shall prosper.

✠ The ungodly *are* not so: but *are* like the chaff which the wind driveth away.

Therefore the ungodly shall not stand in the judgment, nor sinners in the congregation of the righteous.

✠ For the LORD knoweth the way of the righteous: but the way of the ungodly shall perish.

Psalm i. 1-6.

One Hundred and Sixty-eighth Selection.

The Steps of a Good Man.

THE steps of a *good* man are ordered by the LORD: and he delighteth in his way.

✠ Though he fall, he shall not be utterly cast down: for the LORD upholdeth *him with* his hand.

I have been young, and *now* am old;
yet have I not seen the righteous forsaken,
nor his seed begging bread.

✠ *He is* ever merciful, and lendeth; and
his seed *is* blessed.

Depart from evil, and do good; and
dwell for evermore.

✠ For the Lord loveth judgment, and
forsaketh not his saints;

They are preserved for ever: but the
seed of the wicked shall be cut off.

✠ The righteous shall inherit the land,
and dwell therein for ever.

The mouth of the righteous speaketh
wisdom, and his tongue talketh of judgment.

✠ The law of his God *is* in his heart;
none of his steps shall slide.

Psalm xxxvii. 23–31.

One Hundred and Sixty-ninth Selection.

The Righteous shall Endure.

PRAISE ye the Lord. Blessed *is* the
man *that* feareth the Lord, *that* delighteth greatly in his commandments.

✠ His seed shall be mighty upon earth: the generation of the upright shall be blessed.

Wealth and riches *shall be* in his house: and his righteousness endureth for ever.

✠ Unto the upright there ariseth light in the darkness: *he is* gracious, and full of compassion, and righteous.

A good man sheweth favour, and lendeth: he will guide his affairs with discretion.

✠ Surely he shall not be moved for ever: the righteous shall be in everlasting remembrance.

He shall not be afraid of evil tidings: his heart is fixed, trusting in the LORD.

✠ His heart *is* established, he shall not be afraid, until he see *his desire* upon his enemies.

He hath dispersed, he hath given to the poor;

✠ His righteousness endureth for ever; his horn shall be exalted with honour.

The wicked shall see *it*, and be grieved; he shall gnash with his teeth, and melt away: the desire of the wicked shall perish.

Psalm cxii. 1–10.

One Hundred and Seventieth Selection.

Judgment according to Truth.

THEREFORE thou art inexcusable, O man, whosoever thou art, that judgest: for wherein thou judgest another, thou condemnest thyself; for thou that judgest, doest the same things.

✝ But we are sure that the judgment of God is according to truth, against them which commit such things.

And thinkest thou this, O man, that judgest them which do such things, and doest the same, that thou shalt escape the judgment of God?

✝ Or despisest thou the riches of his goodness, and forbearance, and long-suffering; not knowing that the goodness of God leadeth thee to repentance?

But after thy hardness and impenitent heart, treasurest up unto thyself wrath against the day of wrath, and revelation of the righteous judgment of God;

✝ Who will render to every man according to his deeds:

To them who by patient continuance in

well-doing, seek for glory, and honour, and immortality; eternal life:

✠ But unto them that are contentious, and do not obey the truth, but obey unrighteousness; indignation and wrath,

Tribulation and anguish, upon every soul of man that doeth evil; of the Jew first, and also of the Gentile;

✠ But glory, honour, and peace, to every man that worketh good; to the Jew first, and also to the Gentile.

Romans ii. 1-10.

One Hundred and Seventy-first Selection.

The Vanity of Riches.

HEAR this, all *ye* people; give ear, all *ye* inhabitants of the world:

✠ Both low and high, rich and poor, together.

My mouth shall speak of wisdom; and the meditation of my heart *shall be* of understanding.

✠ I will incline mine ear to a parable: I will open my dark saying upon the harp.

They that trust in their wealth, and

boast themselves in the multitude of their riches;

✠ None *of them* can by any means redeem his brother, nor give to God a ransom for him:

For he seeth *that* wise men die, likewise the fool and the brutish person perish, and leave their wealth to others.

✠ Their inward thought *is, that* their houses *shall continue* for ever, *and* their dwelling-places to all generations; they call *their* lands after their own names.

Nevertheless man *being* in honour abideth not: he is like the beasts *that* perish.

✠ Be not thou afraid when one is made rich, when the glory of his house is increased;

For when he dieth he shall carry nothing away: his glory shall not descend after him.

✠ Though while he lived he blessed his soul, (and *men* will praise thee, when thou doest well to thyself,)

He shall go to the generation of his fathers; they shall never see light.

✠ Man *that is* in honour, and understandeth not, is like the beasts *that* perish.

Psalm xlix. 1-4, 6, 7, 10-12, 16-20.

One Hundred and Seventy-second Selection.

The Fulfilling of the Law.

RENDER therefore to all their dues: tribute to whom tribute *is due;* custom to whom custom; fear to whom fear; honour to whom honour.

✠ Owe no man anything, but to love one another: for he that loveth another hath fulfilled the law.

For this, Thou shalt not commit adultery, Thou shalt not kill, Thou shalt not steal, Thou shalt not bear false witness, Thou shalt not covet; and if *there be* any other commandment, it is briefly comprehended in this saying, namely, Thou shalt love thy neighbour as thyself.

✠ Love worketh no ill to his neighbour: therefore love *is* the fulfilling of the law.

And that, knowing the time, that now *it is* high time to awake out of sleep:

✠ For now *is* our salvation nearer than when we believed.

The night is far spent, the day is at hand:

let us therefore cast off the works of darkness, and let us put on the armour of light.

✣ Let us walk honestly, as in the day: not in rioting and drunkenness, not in chambering and wantonness, not in strife and envying.

But put ye on the Lord Jesus Christ, and make not provision for the flesh, to *fulfil* the lusts *thereof*.
Romans xiii. 7-14.

One Hundred and Seventy-third Selection.

Acceptable Sacrifice.

LET *your* conversation *be* without covetousness; *and be* content with such things as ye have: for he hath said, I will never leave thee, nor forsake thee.

✣ So that we may boldly say, The Lord *is* my helper, and I will not fear what man shall do unto me.

Remember them which have the rule over you, who have spoken unto you the word of God: whose faith follow, considering the end of *their* conversation:

✠ Jesus Christ the same yesterday, and to-day, and for ever.

Be not carried about with divers and strange doctrines: for *it is* a good thing that the heart be established with grace; not with meats, which have not profited them that have been occupied therein.

✠ We have an altar, whereof they have no right to eat which serve the tabernacle.

For the bodies of those beasts, whose blood is brought into the sanctuary by the high priest for sin, are burned without the camp.

✠ Wherefore Jesus also, that he might sanctify the people with his own blood, suffered without the gate.

Let us go forth therefore unto him without the camp, bearing his reproach.

✠ For here have we no continuing city, but we seek one to come.

By him therefore let us offer the sacrifice of praise to God continually, that is, the fruit of *our* lips, giving thanks to his name.

✠ But to do good, and to communicate, forget not: for with such sacrifices God is well pleased.

Hebrews xiii. 5-16.

One Hundred and Seventy-fourth Selection.

The Proof of Our Ministry.

WE then, *as* workers together *with him*, beseech *you* also that ye receive not the grace of God in vain.

✟ (For he saith, I have heard thee in a time accepted, and in the day of salvation have I succoured thee: behold, now *is* the accepted time; behold, now *is* the day of salvation.)

Giving no offence in any thing, that the ministry be not blamed:

✟ But in all *things* approving ourselves as the ministers of God, in much patience, in afflictions, in necessities, in distresses,

In stripes, in imprisonments, in tumults, in labours, in watchings, in fastings;

✟ By pureness, by knowledge, by longsuffering, by kindness, by the Holy Ghost, by love unfeigned,

By the word of truth, by the power of God, by the armour of righteousness on the right hand and on the left,

✝ By honour and dishonour, by evil report and good report; as deceivers, and *yet* true;

As unknown, and *yet* well known; as dying, and behold, we live; as chastened, and not killed;

✝ As sorrowful, yet always rejoicing; as poor, yet making many rich; as having nothing, and *yet* possessing all things.
2 *Corinthians* vi. 1-10.

XVIII.

LOVE AND BROTHERHOOD.

―・◇・―

One Hundred and Seventy=fifth Selection.

The Peace of Jerusalem.

I WAS glad when they said unto me, Let us go into the house of the Lord.

✢ Our feet shall stand within thy gates, O Jerusalem.

Jerusalem is builded as a city that is compact together:

✢ Whither the tribes go up, the tribes of the Lord, unto the testimony of Israel, to give thanks unto the name of the Lord.

For there are set thrones of judgment, the thrones of the house of David.

✢ Pray for the peace of Jerusalem: they shall prosper that love thee.

Peace be within thy walls, *and* prosperity within thy palaces.

✢ For my brethren and companions'

sakes, I will now say, Peace *be* within thee.

Because of the house of the LORD our God I will seek thy good.

☩ Behold, how good and how pleasant *it is* for brethren to dwell together in unity!

It is like the precious ointment upon the head, that ran down upon the beard, *even* Aaron's beard: that went down to the skirts of his garments;

☩ As the dew of Hermon, *and as the dew* that descended upon the mountains of Zion: for there the LORD commanded the blessing, *even* life for evermore.

Psalm cxxii. 1–9; cxxxiii. 1–3.

One Hundred and Seventy-sixth Selection.

Unity in Christ.

I THEREFORE, the prisoner of the Lord, beseech you that ye walk worthy of the vocation wherewith ye are called,

☩ With all lowliness and meekness, with long-suffering, forbearing one another in love;

Endeavouring to keep the unity of the Spirit in the bond of peace.

✛ *There is* one body, and one Spirit, even as ye are called in one hope of your calling.

But unto every one of us is given grace according to the measure of the gift of Christ.

✛ Wherefore he saith, When he ascended up on high, he led captivity captive, and gave gifts unto men.

Now that he ascended, what is it but that he also descended first into the lower parts of the earth?

✛ He that descended is the same also that ascended up far above all heavens, that he might fill all things.

And he gave some, apostles; and some, prophets; and some, evangelists; and some, pastors and teachers;

✛ For the perfecting of the saints, for the work of the ministry, for the edifying of the body of Christ:

Till we all come in the unity of the faith, and of the knowledge of the Son of God, unto a perfect man, unto the measure of the stature of the fulness of Christ:

✠ That we *henceforth* be no more children, tossed to and fro, and carried about with every wind of doctrine,

By the sleight of men, *and* cunning craftiness, whereby they lie in wait to deceive:

✠ But speaking the truth in love, may grow up into him in all things, which is the head, *even* Christ:

From whom the whole body fitly joined together and compacted by that which every joint supplieth, according to the effectual working in the measure of every part, maketh increase of the body unto the edifying of itself in love.

Ephesians iv. 1-4, 7-16.

One Hundred and Seventy-seventh Selection.

The Greatest of These is Charity.

THOUGH I speak with the tongues of men and of angels, and have not charity, I am become *as* sounding brass or a tinkling cymbal.

✠ And though I have *the gift of* prophecy, and understand all mysteries, and all knowledge; and though I have all faith, so that I could remove mountains, and have not charity, I am nothing.

And though I bestow all my goods to feed *the poor*, and though I give my body to be burned, and have not charity, it profiteth me nothing.

✢ Charity suffereth long, *and* is kind; charity envieth not; charity vaunteth not itself, is not puffed up,

Doth not behave itself unseemly, seeketh not her own, is not easily provoked, thinketh no evil;

✢ Rejoiceth not in iniquity, but rejoiceth in the truth;

Beareth all things, believeth all things, hopeth all things, endureth all things.

✢ Charity never faileth:

But whether *there be* prophecies, they shall fail; whether *there be* tongues, they shall cease; whether *there be* knowledge, it shall vanish away.

✢ For we know in part, and we prophesy in part.

But when that which is perfect is come, then that which is in part shall be done away.

✠ When I was a child, I spake as a child, I understood as a child, I thought as a child:

But when I became a man, I put away childish things.

✠ For now we see through a glass, darkly; but then face to face:

Now I know in part; but then shall I know even as also I am known.

✠ And now abideth faith, hope, charity, these three; but the greatest of these *is* charity.

1 *Corinthians* xiii. 1-13.

One Hundred and Seventy-eighth Selection.

Love is of God.

BELOVED, let us love one another: for love is of God; and every one that loveth is born of God, and knoweth God.

✠ He that loveth not knoweth not God; for God is love.

In this was manifested the love of God toward us, because that God sent his only begotten Son into the world, that we might live through him.

✢ Herein is love, not that we loved God, but that he loved us, and sent his Son *to be* the propitiation for our sins.

Beloved, if God so loved us, we ought also to love one another.

✢ No man hath seen God at any time. If we love another, God dwelleth in us, and his love is perfected in us.

Hereby know we that we dwell in him, and he in us, because he hath given us of his Spirit.

✢ And we have seen and do testify that the Father sent the Son *to be* the Saviour of the world.

Whosoever shall confess that Jesus is the Son of God, God dwelleth in him, and he in God.

✢ And we have known and believed the love that God hath to us.

God is love; and he that dwelleth in love dwelleth in God, and God in him.

✢ Herein is our love made perfect, that we may have boldness in the day of judgment: because as he is, so are we in this world.

There is no fear in love; but perfect love casteth out fear: because fear hath torment. He that feareth is not made perfect in love.

✢ We love him, because he first loved us.

If a man say, I love God, and hateth his brother, he is a liar: for he that loveth not his brother, whom he hath seen, how can he love God whom he hath not seen?

✢ And this commandment have we from him, That he who loveth God, love his brother also.

1 John iv. 7-21.

One Hundred and Seventy-ninth Selection.

The Sons of God.

BEHOLD, what manner of love the Father hath bestowed upon us, that we should be called the sons of God:

✢ Therefore the world knoweth us not, because it knew him not.

Beloved, now are we the sons of God, and it doth not yet appear what we shall be:

✢ But we know that, when he shall appear, we shall be like him, for we shall see him as he is.

My little children, let us not love in word, neither in tongue; but in deed and in truth.

✣ And hereby we know that we are of the truth, and shall assure our hearts before him.

For if our heart condemn us, God is greater than our heart, and knoweth all things.

✣ Beloved, if our heart condemn us not, *then* have we confidence toward God.

And whatsoever we ask, we receive of him, because we keep his commandments, and do those things that are pleasing in his sight.

✣ And this is his commandment, That we should believe on the name of his Son Jesus Christ, and love one another, as he gave us commandment.

And he that keepeth his commandments dwelleth in him, and he in him.

✣ And hereby we know that he abideth in us, by the Spirit which he hath given us.

1 *John* iii. 1-3, 18-24.

One Hundred and Eightieth Selection.

Members One of Another.

FOR as we have many members in one body, and all members have not the same office:

✠ So we, *being* many, are one body in Christ, and every one members one of another.

Having then gifts differing according to the grace that is given to us, whether prophecy, *let us prophesy* according to the proportion of faith;

✠ Or ministry, *let us wait* on *our* ministering; or he that teacheth, on teaching;

Or he that exhorteth, on exhortation: he that giveth, *let him do it* with simplicity; he that ruleth, with diligence; he that sheweth mercy, with cheerfulness.

✠ *Let* love be without dissimulation. Abhor that which is evil; cleave to that which is good.

Be kindly affectioned one to another with brotherly love; in honour preferring one another.

✠ Not slothful in business; fervent in spirit; serving the Lord;

Rejoicing in hope; patient in tribulation; continuing instant in prayer;

✠ Distributing to the necessity of saints; given to hospitality.

Bless them which persecute you: bless, and curse not.

✠ Rejoice with them that do rejoice, and weep with them that weep.

Be of the same mind one toward another. Mind not high things, but condescend to men of low estate. Be not wise in your own conceits.

✠ Recompense to no man evil for evil. Provide things honest in the sight of all men.

If it be possible, as much as lieth in you, live peaceably with all men.

✠ Dearly beloved, avenge not yourselves, but *rather* give place unto wrath: for it is written, Vengeance *is* mine; I will repay, saith the Lord.

Therefore if thine enemy hunger, feed him; if he thirst, give him drink: for in so doing thou shalt heap coals of fire on his head.

✠ Be not overcome of evil, but overcome evil with good.

Romans xii. 4-21.

XIX.

COUNSELS OF PERFECTION.

One Hundred and Eighty-first Selection.

The Blessings of Jesus.

BLESSED *are* the poor in spirit: for theirs is the kingdom of heaven.

✙ Blessed *are* they that mourn: for they shall be comforted.

Blessed *are* the meek: for they shall inherit the earth.

✙ Blessed *are* they which do hunger and thirst after righteousness: for they shall be filled.

Blessed *are* the merciful: for they shall obtain mercy.

✙ Blessed *are* the pure in heart: for they shall see God.

Blessed *are* the peacemakers: for they shall be called the children of God.

✙ Blessed *are* they which are persecuted for righteousness' sake: for theirs is the kingdom of heaven.

Blessed are ye, when *men* shall revile you, and persecute *you*, and shall say all manner of evil against you falsely, for my sake.

✠ Rejoice, and be exceeding glad: for great *is* your reward in heaven: for so persecuted they the prophets which were before you.   *St. Matthew* v. 3-12.

One Hundred Eighty-second Selection.

The Life of Jesus in Us.

FOR we preach not ourselves, but Christ Jesus the Lord;

✠ And ourselves your servants for Jesus' sake.

For God, who commanded the light to shine out of darkness, hath shined in our hearts,

✠ To *give* the light of the knowledge of the glory of God in the face of Jesus Christ.

But we have this treasure in earthen vessels, that the excellency of the power may be of God and not of us.

✠ *We are* troubled on every side, yet

not distressed; *we are* perplexed, but not in despair;

Persecuted, but not forsaken; cast down, but not destroyed;

✠ Always bearing about in the body the dying of the Lord Jesus, that the life also of Jesus might be made manifest in our body.

For we which live are alway delivered unto death for Jesus' sake, that the life also of Jesus might be made manifest in our mortal flesh.   *2 Corinthians* iv. 5-11.

One Hundred and Eighty-third Selection.

The Mind of Christ.

IF *there be* therefore any consolation in Christ, if any comfort of love, if any fellowship of the Spirit, if any bowels and mercies,

✠ Fulfil ye my joy, that ye be likeminded, having the same love, *being* of one accord, of one mind.

Let nothing *be done* through strife or vainglory; but in lowliness of mind let each esteem other better than themselves.

✧ Look not every man on his own things, but every man also on the things of others.

Let this mind be in you, which was also in Christ Jesus:

✧ Who, being in the form of God, thought it not robbery to be equal with God:

But made himself of no reputation, and took upon him the form of a servant, and was made in the likeness of men:

✧ And being found in fashion as a man, he humbled himself, and became obedient unto death, even the death of the cross.

Wherefore God also hath highly exalted him, and given him a name which is above every name:

✧ That at the name of Jesus every knee should bow, of *things* in heaven, and *things* in earth, and *things* under the earth;

And *that* every tongue should confess that Jesus Christ *is* Lord, to the glory of God the Father.

Philippians ii. 1–11.

One Hundred and Eighty-fourth Selection.

Follow That Which is Good.

SEE that none render evil for evil unto any *man;* but ever follow that which is good, both among yourselves, and to all *men.*

✝ Rejoice evermore. Pray without ceasing.

In every thing give thanks: for this is the will of God in Christ Jesus concerning you.

✝ Quench not the Spirit. Despise not prophesyings.

Prove all things; hold fast that which is good.

✝ Abstain from all appearance of evil.

And the very God of peace sanctify you wholly; and *I pray God* your whole spirit and soul and body be preserved blameless unto the coming of our Lord Jesus Christ.

✝ Faithful *is* he that calleth you, who also will do *it.*

1 *Thessalonians* v. 15–24.

One Hundred and Eighty-fifth Selection.

Be Not Weary in Well Doing.

BRETHREN, if a man be overtaken in a fault, ye which are spiritual, restore such an one in the spirit of meekness; considering thyself, lest thou also be tempted.

✢ Bear ye one another's burdens, and so fulfil the law of Christ.

For if a man think himself to be something, when he is nothing, he deceiveth himself.

✢ But let every man prove his own work, and then shall he have rejoicing in himself alone, and not in another.

For every man shall bear his own burden.

✢ Let him that is taught in the word communicate unto him that teacheth in all good things.

Be not deceived; God is not mocked: for whatsoever a man soweth, that shall he also reap.

✢ For he that soweth to his flesh shall of the flesh reap corruption;

But he that soweth to the Spirit shall of the Spirit reap life everlasting.

✢ And let us not be weary in well doing: for in due season we shall reap, if we faint not.

As we have therefore opportunity, let us do good unto all *men*, especially unto them who are of the household of faith.

Galatians vi. 1–10.

One Hundred and Eighty-sixth Selection.

Truth, Peace, Purity, Forgiveness.

WHEREFORE putting away lying, speak every man truth with his neighbour:

✢ For we are members one of another.

Be ye angry, and sin not: let not the sun go down upon your wrath:

✢ Neither give place to the devil.

Let him that stole steal no more:

✢ But rather let him labour, working with *his* hands the thing which is good, that he may have to give to him that needeth.

Let no corrupt communication proceed out of your mouth,

✠ But that which is good to the use of edifying, that it may minister grace unto the hearers.

And grieve not the Holy Spirit of God, whereby ye are sealed unto the day of redemption.

✠ Let all bitterness, and wrath, and anger, and clamour, and evil speaking, be put away from you, with all malice:

And be ye kind one to another, tenderhearted, forgiving one another, even as God for Christ's sake hath forgiven you.

Ephesians iv. 25-32.

One Hundred and Eighty-seventh Selection.

The Children of Light.

YE are all the children of light, and the children of the day: we are not of the night, nor of darkness.

✠ Therefore let us not sleep, as *do* others; but let us watch and be sober.

For they that sleep sleep in the night; and they that be drunken are drunken in the night.

✠ But let us, who are of the day, be sober, putting on the breastplate of faith and love; and for a helmet, the hope of salvation.

For God hath not appointed us to wrath, but to obtain salvation by our Lord Jesus Christ,

✠ Who died for us, that, whether we wake or sleep, we should live together with him.   1 *Thessalonians* v. 5-10.

One Hundred and Eighty-eighth Selection.

Let Us Glory in the Lord.

WHERE *is* the wise? where *is* the scribe? where *is* the disputer of this world?

✠ Hath not God made foolish the wisdom of this world?

For after that in the wisdom of God the world by wisdom knew not God, it pleased God by the foolishness of preaching to save them that believe.

✠ For the Jews require a sign, and the Greeks seek after wisdom:

But we preach Christ crucified, unto the Jews a stumbling-block, and unto the Greeks foolishness;

✣ But unto them which are called, both jews and Greeks, Christ the power of God, and the wisdom of God.

Because the foolishness of God is wiser than men;

✣ And the weakness of God is stronger than men.

For ye see your calling, brethren, how that not many wise men after the flesh, not many mighty, not many noble, *are called:*

✣ But God hath chosen the foolish things of the world to confound the wise; and God hath chosen the weak things of the world to confound the things which are mighty;

And base things of the world, and things which are despised, hath God chosen, *yea*, and things which are not, to bring to nought things that are:

✣ That no flesh should glory in his presence.

But of him are ye in Christ Jesus, who of God is made unto us wisdom, and righteousness, and sanctification, and redemption:

✠ That, according as it is written, He that glorieth, let him glory in the Lord.
1 *Corinthians* i. 20–31.

One Hundred and Eighty-ninth Selection.

According to Christ Jesus.

WE then that are strong ought to bear the infirmities of the weak, and not to please ourselves.

✠ Let every one of us please *his* neighbour for *his* good to edification.

For even Christ pleased not himself; but, as it is written, The reproaches of them that reproached thee fell on me.

✠ For whatsoever things were written aforetime were written for our learning, that we through patience and comfort of the Scriptures might have hope.

Now the God of patience and consolation grant you to be likeminded one toward another according to Christ Jesus:

✠ That ye may with one mind *and* one mouth glorify God, even the Father of our Lord Jesus Christ.
Romans xv. 1–6.

One Hundred and Ninetieth Selection.

Love and Light.

MY little children, these things write I unto you, that ye sin not. And if any man sin, we have an advocate with the Father, Jesus Christ the righteous:

✢ And he is the propitiation for our sins: and not for ours only, but also for *the sins of* the whole world.

And hereby we do know that we know him, if we keep his commandments.

✢ He that saith, I know him, and keepeth not his commandments, is a liar, and the truth is not in him.

But whoso keepeth his word, in him verily is the love of God perfected: hereby know we that we are in him.

✢ He that saith he abideth in him, ought himself also so to walk, even as he walked.

Brethren, I write no new commandment unto you, but an old commandment which ye had from the beginning:

✢ The old commandment is the word which ye have heard from the beginning.

Again, a new commandment I write unto you, which thing is true in him and in you:

✠ Because the darkness is past, and the true light now shineth.

He that saith he is in the light, and hateth his brother, is in darkness even until now.

✠ He that loveth his brother abideth in the light, and there is none occasion of stumbling in him.

But he that hateth his brother is in darkness, and walketh in darkness, and knoweth not whither he goeth, because that darkness hath blinded his eyes.

1 *John* ii. 1-11.

One Hundred and Ninety-first Selection.

Consider Christ.

WHEREFORE, holy brethren, partakers of the heavenly calling, consider the Apostle and High Priest of our profession, Christ Jesus;

✠ Who was faithful to him that appointed him, as also Moses *was faithful* in all his house.

For this *man* was counted worthy of more glory than Moses, inasmuch as he who hath builded the house, hath more honour than the house.

✠ For every house is builded by some *man*; but he that built all things *is* God.

And Moses verily *was* faithful in all his house, as a servant, for a testimony of those things which were to be spoken after:

✠ But Christ as a Son over his own house: whose house are we, if we hold fast the confidence, and the rejoicing of the hope firm unto the end.

Wherefore, as the Holy Ghost saith, To-day if ye will hear his voice,

✠ Harden not your hearts, as in the provocation, in the day of temptation in the wilderness:

When your fathers tempted me, proved me, and saw my works forty years.

✠ Wherefore I was grieved with that generation, and said, They do always err in *their* heart; and they have not known my ways.

So I sware in my wrath, They shall not enter into my rest.

✠ Take heed, brethren, lest there be in any of you an evil heart of unbelief, in departing from the living God.

But exhort one another daily, while it is called To-day; lest any of you be hardened through the deceitfulness of sin.

✠ For we are made partakers of Christ, if we hold the beginning of our confidence steadfast unto the end.

Hebrews iii. 1-14.

XX.

THE RISEN LIFE.

One Hundred and Ninety-second Selection.

Now is Christ Risen from the Dead.

IF in this life only we have hope in Christ, we are of all men most miserable.

✠ But now is Christ risen from the dead, *and* become the firstfruits of them that slept.

For since by man *came* death, by man *came* also the resurrection of the dead.

✠ For as in Adam all die, even so in Christ shall all be made alive.

But every man in his own order: Christ the firstfruits;

✠ Afterward they that are Christ's at his coming.

Then *cometh* the end, when he shall have delivered up the kingdom to God, even the Father;

✢ When he shall have put down all rule and all authority and power.

For he must reign, till he hath put all enemies under his feet.

✢ The last enemy that shall be destroyed is death.

For he hath put all things under his feet.

✢ But when he saith all things are put under *him, it is* manifest that he is excepted, which did put all things under him.

And when all things shall be subdued unto him, then shall the Son also himself be subject unto him that put all things under him, that God may be all in all.

1 *Corinthians* xv. 19-28.

One Hundred and Ninety-third Selection.

Risen with Christ.

IF ye then be risen with Christ, seek those things which are above, where Christ sitteth on the right hand of God.

✢ Set your affection on things above, not on things on the earth.

For ye are dead, and your life is hid with Christ in God.

✠ When Christ, *who is* our life, shall appear, then shall ye also appear with him in glory.

Mortify therefore your members which are upon the earth; fornication, uncleanness, inordinate affection, evil concupiscence, and covetousness, which is idolatry:

✠ For which things' sake the wrath of God cometh on the children of disobedience:

In the which ye also walked sometime, when ye lived in them.

✠ But now ye also put off all these; anger, wrath, malice, blasphemy, filthy communication out of your mouth.

Lie not one to another, seeing that ye have put off the old man with his deeds;

✠ And have put on the new *man*, which is renewed in knowledge after the image of him that created him:

Where there is neither Greek nor Jew, circumcision nor uncircumcision, Barbarian, Scythian, bond *nor* free:

✠ But Christ *is* all, and in all.

Put on therefore, as the elect of God,

holy and beloved, bowels of mercies, kindness, humbleness of mind, meekness, longsuffering;

✠ Forbearing one another and forgiving one another, if any man have a quarrel against any: even as Christ forgave you, so also *do* ye.

And above all these things *put on* charity, which is the bond of perfectness.

✠ And let the peace of God rule in your hearts, to the which also ye are called in one body; and be ye thankful.

Let the word of Christ dwell in you richly in all wisdom; teaching and admonishing one another in psalms and hymns and spiritual songs, singing with grace in your hearts to the Lord.

✠ And whatsoever ye do in word or deed, *do* all in the name of the Lord Jesus, giving thanks to God and the Father by him.

Colossians iii. 1–17.

One Hundred and Ninety-fourth Selection.

In Newness of Life.

WHAT shall we say then? Shall we continue in sin, that grace may abound?

✠ God forbid. How shall we, that are dead to sin, live any longer therein?

Know ye not, that so many of us as were baptized into Jesus Christ were baptized into his death?

✠ Therefore we are buried with him by baptism into death:

That like as Christ was raised up from the dead by the glory of the Father, even so we also should walk in newness of life.

✠ For if we have been planted together in the likeness of his death, we shall be also *in the likeness* of *his* resurrection:

Knowing this, that our old man is crucified with *him*, that the body of sin might be destroyed, that henceforth we should not serve sin.

✠ For he that is dead is freed from sin.

Now if we be dead with Christ, we believe that we shall also live with him:

✙ Knowing that Christ being raised from the dead dieth no more; death hath no more dominion over him.

For in that he died, he died unto sin once: but in that he liveth, he liveth unto God.

Romans vi. 1-10.

One Hundred and Ninety-fifth Selection.

A Lively Hope.

BLESSED *be* the God and Father of our Lord Jesus Christ, which according to his abundant mercy hath begotten us again into a lively hope by the resurrection of Jesus Christ from the dead,

✙ To an inheritance incorruptible, and undefiled, and that fadeth not away, reserved in heaven for you,

Who are kept by the power of God through faith unto salvation ready to be revealed in the last time.

✙ Wherein ye greatly rejoice, though now for a season, if need be, ye are in heaviness through manifold temptations:

That the trial of your faith, being much more precious than of gold that perisheth, though it be tried with fire, might be found unto praise and honour and glory at the appearing of Jesus Christ:

✠ Whom, having not seen, ye love; in whom, though now ye see *him* not, yet believing, ye rejoice with joy unspeakable and full of glory:

Receiving the end of your faith, even the salvation of *your* souls.

✠ Now unto the King, eternal, immortal, invisible, the only wise God, *be* honour and glory for ever and ever. Amen.

1 *Peter* i. 3–9; 1 *Timothy* i. 17.

One Hundred and Ninety-sixth Selection.

The Victory over Death.

NOW this I say, brethren, that flesh and blood cannot inherit the kingdom of God; neither doth corruption inherit incorruption.

✠ Behold, I shew you a mystery; We shall not all sleep, but we shall all be changed,

In a moment, in the twinkling of an eye, at the last trump: for the trumpet shall sound, and the dead shall be raised incorruptible, and we shall be changed.

✚ For this corruptible must put on incorruption, and this mortal *must* put on immortality.

So when this corruptible shall have put on incorruption, and this mortal shall have put on immortality, then shall be brought to pass the saying that is written, Death is swallowed up in victory.

✚ O death, where *is* thy sting? O grave, where *is* thy victory?

The sting of death *is* sin; and the strength of sin *is* the law.

✚ But thanks *be* to God, which giveth us the victory through our Lord Jesus Christ.

Therefore, my beloved brethren, be ye steadfast, unmovable, always abounding in the work of the Lord, forasmuch as ye know that your labour is not in vain in the Lord.

1 *Corinthians* xv. 50–58.

One Hundred and Ninety-seventh Selection.

Our House Which is from Heaven.

FOR we know that if our earthly house of *this* tabernacle were dissolved, we have a building of God, an house not made with hands, eternal in the heavens.

✢ For in this we groan, earnestly desiring to be clothed upon with our house which is from heaven:

If so be that being clothed we shall not be found naked.

✢ For we that are in *this* tabernacle do groan, being burdened:

Not for that we would be unclothed, but clothed upon, that mortality might be swallowed up of life.

✢ Now he that hath wrought us for the selfsame thing *is* God, who also hath given unto us the earnest of the Spirit.

Therefore *we are* always confident, knowing that, whilst we are at home in the body, we are absent from the Lord:

✢ (For we walk by faith, not by sight:)

We are confident, *I say*, and willing rather to be absent from the body, and to be present with the Lord.

✠ Wherefore we labour, that, whether present or absent, we may be accepted of him.

2 *Corinthians* v. 1–9.

One Hundred and Ninety-eighth Selection.

The Blessedness of the Redeemed.

AFTER this I beheld, and lo, a great multitude, which no man could number, of all nations, and kindreds, and people, and tongues, stood before the throne, and before the Lamb, clothed with white robes, and palms in their hands;

✠ And cried with a loud voice, saying, Salvation to our God which sitteth upon the throne, and unto the Lamb.

And all the angels stood round about the throne, and *about* the elders and the four beasts, and fell before the throne on their faces, and worshipped God,

✠ Saying, Amen: Blessing, and glory, and wisdom, and thanksgiving, and honour, and power, and might, *be* unto our God for ever and ever. Amen.

And one of the elders answered, saying unto me, What are these which are arrayed in white robes? and whence came they? And I said unto him, Sir, thou knowest.

✚ And he said to me, These are they which came out of great tribulation, and have washed their robes, and made them white in the blood of the Lamb.

Therefore are they before the throne of God, and serve him day and night in his temple: and he that sitteth on the throne shall dwell among them.

✚ They shall hunger no more, neither thirst any more; neither shall the sun light on them, nor any heat.

For the Lamb which is in the midst of the throne shall feed them, and shall lead them unto living fountains of waters: and God shall wipe away all tears from their eyes.

Revelation vii. 9-17.

One Hundred and Ninety-ninth Selection.

The Holy City.

A ND I saw a new heaven and a new earth:

✢ For the first heaven and the first earth were passed away; and there was no more sea.

And I John saw the holy city, new Jerusalem, coming down from God out of heaven, prepared as a bride adorned for her husband.

✢ And I heard a great voice out of heaven, saying, Behold, the tabernacle of God *is* with men, and he will dwell with them, and they shall be his people, and God himself shall be with them, *and be* their God.

And God shall wipe away all tears from their eyes; and there shall be no more death, neither sorrow, nor crying, neither shall there be any more pain: for the former things have passed away.

✢ And I saw no temple therein: for the Lord God Almighty and the Lamb are the temple of it.

And the city had no need of the sun, neither of the moon, to shine in it: for the glory of God did lighten it, and the Lamb *is* the light thereof.

✠ And the nations of them which are saved shall walk in the light of it: and the kings of the earth do bring their glory and honour into it.

And the gates of it shall not be shut at all by day: for there shall be no night there.

✠ And they shall bring the glory and honour of the nations into it.

And there shall in no wise enter into it any thing that defileth, neither *whatsoever* worketh abomination, or *maketh* a lie; but they which are written in the Lamb's book of life.

Revelation xxi. 1–4, 22–27.

Two Hundredth Selection.

The River of Water of Life.

AND he shewed me a pure river of water of life, clear as crystal, proceeding out of the throne of God and of the Lamb.

✠ In the midst of the street of it, and on either side of the river, *was there* the tree of life,

Which bare twelve *manner of* fruits, *and* yielded her fruit every month:

✠ And the leaves of the tree *were* for the healing of the nations.

And there shall be no more curse: but the throne of God and of the Lamb shall be in it;

✠ And his servants shall serve him: and they shall see his face; and his name *shall be* in their foreheads.

And there shall be no night there; and they need no candle, neither light of the sun;

✠ For the Lord God giveth them light: and they shall reign for ever and ever.

And he said unto me, These sayings *are* faithful and true:

✠ And the Lord God of the holy prophets sent his angel to shew unto his servants the things which must shortly be done.

Behold, I come quickly: blessed *is* he that keepeth the sayings of the prophecy of this book.

✟ And the Spirit and the bride say, Come. And let him that heareth say, Come.

And let him that is athirst come. And whosoever will, let him take the **water of life** freely.

Revelation xxii. 1–7, 17.

INDEX OF BIBLE PASSAGES.

	PASSAGE	SELECTION	PAGE
Deut.	viii. 1, 6–18	156	242
	xi. 1, 13–21	157	244
	xxviii. 1–10	158	246
	xxxii. 1–12	41	64
2 Sam.	xxii. 21–29	164	254
1 Chron.	xvi. 8–15	118	186
	23–36	4	4
Job	xi. 7–18	50	78
	xxii. 12–30	142	219
	xxviii. 12–28	52	81
Psalm	i. 1–6	167	258
	ii. 1–12	58	91
	iv. 1–8	137	213
	v. 1–8; 11, 12	48	75
	viii. 1–9	12	18
	xiii. 1–6	134	209
	xv. 1–5	162	252
	xvi. 1–11	120	189
	xviii. 1–3; 20–28	145	224
	30–36; 46–50	130	203
	xix. 1–14	17	26
	xx. 1–9	134	209
	xxi. 1–7; 31	32	51
	xxii. 22–13	44	68
	xxiii. 1–6	115	182

	PASSAGE	SELECTION	PAGE
Psalm	xxiv. 1–10	13	20
	xxv. 1–14	108	171
	xxvi. 1–12	161	251
	xxvii. 1–14	148	229
	xxx. 1–12	136	211
	xxxi. 1–8; 19–24	129	201
	xxxii. 1–11	113	178
	xxxiii. 1–12	45	70
	13–22	143	221
	xxxiv. 1–22	39	60
	xxxvi. 5–10	31	50
	xxxvii. 1–11	166	257
	23–31	168	259
	xxxix. 1–13	109	173
	xl. 1–11	133	207
	xlii. 1–11	155	240
	xliii. 1–5	149	231
	xlv. 1–17	60	94
	xlvi. 1–11	127	198
	xlvii. 1–9	16	24
	xlviii. 1–14	76	123
	xlix. 1–4, 6, 7, 10–12, 16–20	171	263
	l. 1–15	88	145
	li. 1–4, 9–17	104	106
	lvi. 1–13	34	53
	lvii. 1–11	37	58
	lxi. 1–8	139	216
	lxii. 1–12	140	217
	lxv. 1–13	26	40
	lxvi. 1–9, 16–20	35	54
	lxvii. 1–7	5	6
	lxviii. 1–8, 32–35	15	22
	lxxii. 1–19	61	96

PASSAGE	SELECTION	PAGE
Psalm lxxxiv. 1–12	126	196
lxxxv. 1–13	112	177
lxxxvi. 1–12	131	204
lxxxix. 1–7	40	63
8–18	42	66
xc. 1–17	57	88
xci. 1–16	138	214
xcii. 1–8, 12–15	123	192
xciii. 1–5	128	199
xcv. 1–11	43	67
xcvi. 1–13	14	21
xcvii. 1–12	6	7
xcviii. 1–9	2	2
xcix. 1–9	19	29
c. 1–5	49	76
ci. 1–8	159	248
cii. 1, 2, 16–28	144	222
ciii. 1–22	30	47
civ. 1–24	11	16
cv. 1–8, 43–45	27	42
cvi. 1–8, 43–48	24	37
cvii. 1–15	21	32
21–31	25	39
31–43	22	34
cxi. 1–10	18	28
cxii. 1–10	169	260
cxv. 1–18	7	8
cxvi. 1–19	36	56
cxviii. 1–6, 19–26	29	46
cxix. 1–16	91	150
17–24	92	151
25–32	93	152
33–48	20	30

	PASSAGE	SELECTION	PAGE
Psalm	cxix. 49–64	94	153
	65–80	95	155
	89–96	96	156
	97–106	97	157
	107–117	111	176
	124–133	98	158
	137–144	99	159
	145–160	100	160
	161–168	101	162
	169–176	102	163
	cxxi. 1–8	141	218
	cxxii. 1–9 and cxxxiii. 1–3	175	270
	cxxiii.	132	206
	cxxiv.	132	206
	cxxv. 1–5	128	199
	cxxvi.	117	184
	cxxix.	117	184
	cxxxi. 1–3	149	231
	cxxx. 1–8	105	167
	cxxxii. 1–18	160	249
	cxxxiii. 1–30	175	270
	cxxxv. 1–5, 15–21	10	14
	cxxxvi. 1–26	28	43
	cxxxviii. 1–8	33	52
	cxxxix. 1–12, 23, 24	51	79
	cxlii. 1–7	135	210
	cxliii. 1–11	110	174
	cxliv. 1–15	146	226
	cxlv. 1–21	23	35
	cxlvi. 1–10	38	59
	cxlvii. 1–20	47	73
	cxlviii. 1–14	1	1
	cxlix. 1–4	49	76

Index of Bible Passages.

	PASSAGE	SELECTION	PAGE
Psalm	cl. 1–6	3	4
Prov.	ii. 1–9	53	82
	iii. 13–26	54	83
	iv. 1–13	56	87
	14–27	165	256
	viii. 1–21	55	85
	xxii. 1–12	163	253
Isaiah	i. 2, 11, 13–20	64	101
	ix. 2, 6, 7	65	102
	xi. 1–6	72	115
	1–9	65	102
	xxv. 1–9	46	71
	xxxv. 1–10	78	125
	xl. 1–11	70	112
	18–31	8	10
	xlii. 1–12, 16	66	104
	xlix. 7–13	74	119
	lii. 7–15	71	114
	liii. 1–12	68	108
	liv. 11–17	77	124
	lv. 1–13	81	131
	lviii. 1–9	87	143
	lx. 1–5, 17–22	79	127
	lxi. 1–11	73	117
	lxii. 1–4, 10, 12	121	190
	lxiv. 1–10	106	168
Hosea	xiv. 1–9	103	164
Joel	ii. 21–27	119	187
Matt.	v. 3–12	181	281
Luke	i. 46–55	62	99
	68–75	63	100
Acts	xvii. 24–31	9	12
Romans	ii. 1–10	170	262

PASSAGE	SELECTION	PAGE
Romans iii. 19–26	114	180
v. 1–11	125	195
vi. 1–10	194	300
viii. 1–11	83	136
16–28	82	134
31–39	116	183
x. 4–15	80	129
xii. 4–21	180	279
xiii. 7–14	172	265
xv. 1–6	189	291
1 Cor. i. 20–31	188	289
xii. 4–13	86	141
xiii. 1–13	177	273
xv. 19–28	192	296
50–58	196	302
2 Cor. iii. 7–18	84	137
iv. 5–11	182	282
13–18	124	193
v. 1–9	197	304
6–9; 14–21	151	234
vi. 1–10	174	268
Gal. v. 13–25	85	139
vi. 1–10	185	286
Eph. ii. 11–22	75	121
iii. 20, 21	116	183
iv. 1–4; 7–16	176	271
25–32	186	287
vi. 10–18	147	228
Phil. iv. 4–8	122	191
ii. 1–11	183	283
Col. i. 9–20	67	106
iii. 1–17	193	297
1 Thess. v. 1–10	150	233

Index of Bible Passages.

PASSAGE		SELECTION	PAGE
1 Thess.	v. 5–10	187	288
	15–24	184	285
Heb.	i. 1–12	59	92
	ii. 5–12	69	110
	iii. 1–14	191	293
	iv. 9–16	153	238
	x. 16–25	154	239
	xii. 1–6; 11–14	152	236
	xiii. 5–16	173	266
James	i. 16–27	89	146
1 Peter	i. 3–9; 17	195	301
2 Peter	i. 2–11	90	148
1 John	i. 5–9	107	170
	ii. 1–11	190	292
	iii. 1–3; 18–24	179	277
	iv. 7–21	178	275
Jude	24, 25	124	193
Rev.	vii. 9–17	198	305
	xxi. 1–4; 22–27	199	307
	xxii. 1–7; 17	200	308

www.ingramcontent.com/pod-product-compliance
Lightning Source LLC
Chambersburg PA
CBHW030006240426
43672CB00007B/844